THE HITTER'S DISCIPLINE:

A Mental Performance Guide for the Baseball Player

Ronnie Ortegon

© 2018 Ronnie Ortegon
All rights reserved.

No part of this publication may be reproduced, stored in a retrieval system, or transmitted, in any form or by any means, electronic, mechanical, photocopying, recording, or otherwise, without the written permission of the author.

First published by Dog Ear Publishing
4011 Vincennes Road
Indianapolis, IN 46268
www.dogearpublishing.net

dog ear
PUBLISHING

ISBN: 978-145756-420-8

This book is printed on acid-free paper.

Printed in the United States of America

Foreword by former Texas Rangers, Houston Astros and Chicago Cubs Hitting Coach Rudy Jaramillo

For 22 years, I had the pleasure of working with some of the greatest players in the Major Leagues during that time period (1990-2012), including names such as Craig Biggio, Jeff Bagwell, Juan Gonzáles, Adrian Gonzalez, Iván "Pudge" Rodríguez, Mark Teixeira, Michael Young, Alfonso Soriano and Anthony Rizzo. Biggio, Bagwell and Pudge have all been inducted into the Hall of Fame, and one or two other players from those teams have a chance, as well.

Here's the thing about baseball, though: Even the best of the best players in the history of the game are going to struggle from time to time with their consistency at the plate. Every player goes through slumps; every hitter must deal with frustrations; and every player who has ever worn an MLB uniform and stepped into the batter's box of an MLB game can benefit from the positive feedback and constructive instruction of a good hitting coach.

That's because hitting a baseball is probably the most difficult thing to consistently do in all of sports. A good hitting coach can keep you in rhythm or pull you out of a funk. A good hitting coach can build up your confidence, elevate your batting average, enhance your outlook and change your approach. A good hitting coach can be a team's best behind-the-scenes secret weapon, and I am proud to endorse the author of this book, Ronnie Ortegon, as a really good hitting coach.

Ronnie has a passion for the game, the art of hitting and helping others. I worked with him during my tenure with the Rangers, and we talked hitting all the time. Hitting the ball consistently well is so much more of a mental discipline than a physical skill, and Ronnie is really good in helping players to understand that because he communicates with players and wins their trust. He's a professional hitting coach, and he is going to teach you a professional approach whether you are on the brink of making it to "the show" or you are preparing for the Little League All-Stars.

Ronnie has proven to be able to build a rapport with pro players, and when you read this book, you will receive the same kind of insights that he shares with his pro players. He is a mechanic, a technician and a psychologist all in one.

Perhaps the only thing more difficult than hitting a baseball is teaching that art, but I can assure you that Ronnie Ortegon knows how to teach it. If I was an aspiring young player, I wouldn't just read this book; I would devour it over and over again.

Introduction

Picture this: It's the bottom of the ninth inning, Game Seven of the World Series, the College World Series, your high school state championship game or whatever you dream about in your ideal baseball scenario.

There's one out with runners at second and third and your team trails by a single run. From the on-deck circle, you watch intensely as the opposing manager walks slowly toward the mound and you begin to realize that his plan likely involves issuing an intentional walk to your teammate—the red-hot contact hitter who is right in front of you in the lineup—to set up the double play possibility. After all, you've already grounded into a double play earlier in the evening, and you were called out on strikes in your other two trips to the plate.

Besides, this particular closer has almost always given you fits, as your career batting average against him is closer to your body temperature than even the Mendoza Line. Momentarily, a thought flashes across your mind, probably the same thought going through the minds of 50,000 people inside this sold-out stadium, as well as millions of fans watching on national television and your own manager: *Do you have what it takes or would a pinch hitter be a better option right now?*

Following the intentional walk that you predicted, your moment of truth has arrived. Your manager has decided to stick with you, and whatever happens next will be the defining point of an entire lifetime of dreams—a memory that could forever bring you joy. Or one that could possibly plague your thoughts forevermore. Succeed or fail. Dog pile or dejection. Hero or zero.

You've been dreaming of this opportunity—this pressure-packed, do-or-die moment in the national spotlight of the national pastime—since your father first placed a plastic bat into your hands as a chubby-faced, diaper-wearing toddler. The chill of the brisk, late-October breeze slicing across the diamond has nothing to do with the goose bumps forming on the back of your neck as you stroll toward the plate. Your walk-up song plays triumphantly and encouragingly over the stadium's speakers as you begin to hear the crowd chant your name. You can practically feel the crowd's energy as you dig your spikes into the back of the batter's box. Not even in your best backyard imaginary games as a child had you ever envisioned the sheer magnitude of this moment.

Now that I have painted this dream-like scenario for you, I really want you to place yourself in that position. Don't just keep reading. Pause. Visualize yourself in your favorite Major League team's uniform (or college or high school) inside that team's home stadium on a cool, crisp October night. You see the glow of the stadium lights in the dark night sky. The flags are fluttering in the breeze above the top of the outfield wall, and every fan in the stadium is on his or her feet for this moment, chewing fingernails, crossing fingers, grasping lucky charms and sending prayers on your behalf. Hear your name being announced to the crowd; listen for your walk-up song; smell the crispness of a perfect fall night; tighten the Velcro straps on your batting gloves; roll the handle of your Louisville Slugger in the fingertips of your hands; and focus so intently on the mound that you can identify the longest whisker on the reliever's goatee. Close your eyes now if necessary to visualize every detail of you in that moment.

Now, that you've placed yourself in that moment, here are my questions: What is that little voice inside your head telling you? How many things are going through your head? Is your heart racing? Or is the beat inside your chest steady? Do you relish this moment? Or do you wish the pinch hitter was in your shoes?

Ultimately, what is going through your own mind is going to play the biggest role in determining your ability to succeed in that scenario…or in any other situation at any other level of baseball. Whether you are hitting at the bottom of your Little League lineup or in the heart of the order for the World Series contenders, your own inner voice is the most vital one to hear, to control and to master. And that's one of the most important things I can teach you in the ensuing pages of this book.

Throughout the years, I have helped many players of various backgrounds and varying talent levels to become outstanding hitters by being mechanically sound, sticking to a game plan and controlling the voice inside their own heads. During my time in and around baseball, I learned from some of the greatest minds in the game including former Philadelphia Phillies and Cleveland Indians manager Charlie Manuel, former Toronto Blue Jays hitting coach Brook Jacoby, Cincinnati Reds hitting coach Donnie Long, Reds coach Tony Jaramillo, former Major League outfielder and former Reds Minor League hitting coordinator Ryan Jackson, longtime friend and multi-sport high school coach Sam Gillispie, former Baylor outfielder Robbie Nicholson, college roommate Tommy Hernandez, who I helped co-found the Dallas Tigers, and legendary former Texas Rangers, Houston Astros and Chicago Cubs hitting instructor Rudy Jaramillo, who provided the foreword for this book. Those men, as well as many others, have had a powerful influence on my career and my life. I've learned so much from them, and I would not be in position to author this book if not for their tremendous guidance and assistance. Nor would I be any kind of authority on the hitter's discipline without my own struggles against the voice inside my own head.

Some of the greatest players throughout history who have gone on to become managers or coaches have had a difficult time relating to players because the game came so easily and naturally to them. It's not easy for some of the great former players to coach "normal" or average players, because so many of the outstanding former players are so extraordinarily gifted that they really don't relate to the struggles, obstacles, doubts and fears that many of us encounter when attempting one of the most difficult things in sports: squarely hitting a round ball with a round bat. Conversely, some of the more mediocre ballplayers actually make great coaches because they recognize their own shortfalls and can easily identify with players who cannot merely rely on God-given abilities or freakish physical giftedness.

I definitely fall into the latter category, which is probably why I have had such a great deal of success helping other players to be successful hitters. I say that humbly, not boastfully, because I have discovered that my gift is in helping others develop, refine and improve their approach, discipline, swing and results when stepping into the batter's box. Quite frankly, this was never my dream or my aspiration. Like so many other boys, I had dreamed of being able to hit on an elite level in the Major Leagues.

Growing up in Plainview, Texas—a small town of about 20,000 residents, roughly 45 minutes north of Lubbock—I first began to fall in love with the game at about the age of four. And from the time I can remember, I always wanted to be just like my older brothers, who both played baseball. We spent countless summer days and numerous post-school afternoons playing baseball with neighborhood kids and my brothers' older friends. Being six to seven years younger than my siblings, I was typically the runt of most neighborhood games. As such, I was usually the last player chosen when dividing into teams. But at least I was chosen, and I would usually end up on my older brothers' team by default.

The old, beat-up wooden bats we used during those games were normally too big and heavy for me, which meant I had to choke way up on the handle just to be able to at least hold it in the proper position, and actually swinging it was a completely different story. Nonetheless, I managed to barrel-up the ball most of the time, even if the power supply was lacking.

As a left-hander, the more difficult challenge in those neighborhood games was fielding. I didn't have my own glove, so I usually had to use one of the other boys' gloves, which really wouldn't have been much of a problem if any of the other boys were left-handed. Unfortunately for me, I was usually the only left-hander, which resulted in me turning the right-handed glove backward and doing my best to catch the ball with the back of the glove. It wasn't until I played on my first youth league team that I finally was able to use a glove specifically for a left hander. As you can imagine, it made a world of a difference, as I went from the bumbling, backward glove boy to the slick-fielding lefty. It certainly helps in baseball and all other walks of life, for that matter, to use the right tools of the trade.

Those early youth league days is where my desire to be a Major Leaguer started. In those days, baseball fans typically only had one nationally televised game each week, which was often on Saturday afternoons. I truly planned my weekends around the NBC Game of the Week, which was broadcast by some combination of Curt Gowdy, Joe Garagiola, Tony Kubek, Vin Scully and Bob Costas. My favorite team growing up was the Milwaukee Brewers, who moved from Seattle to Milwaukee in the early 1970s and didn't have a winning season until the late '70s. I started really paying attention to Milwaukee in 1978 under new manager George Bamberger, a former pitching coach with the Baltimore Orioles. Bamberger immediately turned the team into pennant contenders in '78, as Milwaukee won 93 games with a combination of home-grown players like Robin Yount, Paul Molitor, and Gorman Thomas, as well as cast-offs from other teams like Ben Oglivie, Mike Caldwell and my personal favorite, the great Cecil Cooper.

Cooper, who was also a left-handed hitter, was my favorite guy in the powerful lineup, which became known as "Bambi's Bombers" in reference to George Bamberger. I would imitate Cooper's open, crouched-over, batting stance, mimicking everything about him, especially the way he rested his bat on his shoulder, parallel to the ground. Cooper, who was born in Brenham, Texas and played collegiately at Prairie View A&M, was a five-time All-Star and a terrific hitter. Cooper hit .300 or more every year from 1977-83, including his career-high .352 average in 1980, which was second in the American League behind George Brett (.390), who flirted with .400 throughout the year. I loved watching Cooper, as well as every other game that was broadcast. I would watch the entire game and at the conclusion, I would go outside and pick up tiny pebbles that covered every square inch of our gravel driveway and throw one at a time into the air as I essentially played soft toss with pea gravel. I would pretend to be Joe Garagiola broadcasting Cecil Cooper's at-bat, tossing the pebble into the air, swinging the bat and driving the pebble into the yard as I simulated different game situations. Little did I know then that I was actually performing a good hitting drill by squaring up pea-sized pebbles.

At least that was my routine when I was by myself. As I grew older, our sandlot games were played on a strip of grass that was bordered by neighborhood fences, and behind all of those fences were backyards that contained dogs. Question: Have you ever seen the magnificent 1993 movie, *The Sandlot*? If so, you will definitely recall the canine star of the show, Beast, a massive English Mastiff. We didn't have to contend with any dogs that intimidating, but the bottom line was that if you hit a ball into a backyard you often didn't see it again. And if you did see it again, it was never in as good of condition. There was also another yard that was a forbidden area in centerfield, so you couldn't hit it too far. You just had to hit the ball on a line so that it would bounce off the fences. Out of necessity and by pure blind luck, we all became line-drive hitters, which is exactly what I want to teach the players I work with today!

I often felt blessed with the ability I had to be a hitter who could hit line drives to all fields. I never really struggled as a hitter at any time during my childhood (especially after I grew into the bigger bats). My coach at the time, John Hill, was a man of great faith…and great discipline. He was extremely tough on his players, and his focus was to make us mentally tough at all costs. The most powerful thing we learned from Coach Hill, however, was the power of visualization. He demanded that we visualized every aspect of the game on a consistent basis, especially as we traveled to games on bus trips. He brought out the best in all of us, and led our baseball team to the playoffs for the first time in school history. I learned a great deal about the game and the power of visualization from Coach Hill, who believed that you could prepare yourself for anything you might encounter on the baseball diamond by visualizing it in advance and planning your reaction.

My success under Coach Hill in high school allowed me to play collegiate baseball at Lubbock Christian University and Grand Canyon University. At both schools, I had a great deal of success, especially as a hitter. That's not to say that I didn't have my occasional struggles. I absolutely did, but I really never lost my composure or confidence, and I certainly did not fall victim to panic or anxiety. In fact, I had enough success at small schools at the collegiate level that I signed as a free agent with the California Angels.

At that time, the Angels' hitting coordinator was Joe Maddon. He has proven to be one of the great managers in the modern-day Major Leagues, as Maddon had some great seasons from 2006-14 with Tampa Bay and has—at the time of this writing—continued to do great things with the Chicago Cubs, including leading the Cubs to the 2016 World Series title. The championship was the Cubs' first since 1908, ending the longest world championship drought in North American professional sports history. Maddon is the perfect example of a great coach who wasn't necessarily a great player. Maddon was signed by the Angels organization as a player in 1975 after graduating from Lafayette College. In 1979, after spending four seasons trying to make it as a catcher in the Angels' organization, Maddon gave up his playing career and become a coach. It was a wise decision. He started as a scout, and would continue to climb the coaching ladder in the organization. He was the hitting coordinator when our paths crossed, and he had watched me play a college game in the spring of 1988.

It was there that I must have made an impression on him because he recommended me when they needed to sign a first baseman. During the fall instructional league in 1988, I was on my way to a tryout for a team in Mexico when Maddon contacted me about signing. While on a layover in Phoenix, Joe Maddon, in full uniform, met me in the lobby of the airport terminal, where I signed my first pro contract. That would have made a great movie scene if I had only gone on to become the next Cecil Cooper. Or, sticking with the Angels' organization, the next Rod Carew, Wally Joyner or Kendrys Morales. Unfortunately, that was not meant to be.

I began my professional career in Palm Springs, California, hitting third in the lineup at the start of the season. This is when I first realized the importance of staying in the moment and committing to a game plan. For two years and three spring trainings of pro baseball, I never figured out how to fully commit to a game plan to accomplish what needed to be done. I tried everything, but I simply didn't know how to fix myself.

And here's the big kicker: The problem was NEVER really my swing or my mechanics. I felt like I had a really good, sound swing. The problem was my complete inability to control my mind or that little annoying, questioning voice in my head. I relied on hope, as in, *"Man, I hope I get a hit today."*

I also turned to God, praying that I would get a hit today. For example, *"Dear Heavenly Father, thank you for all my blessings, talents and abilities. And thank you for allowing me to play the game I love. But would you please help me to find a gap here or there?"*

Obviously, the pitchers I was facing had a better relationship at the time with God than I did. That's a joke.

But the point is that I reached a level of desperation where I really was pleading with God for more base hits. Writing that is a little embarrassing, but I am being completely honest here.

Lastly, I relied on superstition, which is even more embarrassing. This was my line of thinking: *"If I wear the same socks and shirt I got a hit with last week, I might get a hit today."*

One of my teammates at the time was Chad Curtis. For an entire season, I watched Chad hit line drives all over the field, and it seemed like he never made an out. No wonder that that he made it to the Majors and played from 1992-2001 with the Angels, Tigers, Dodgers, Indians, Yankees and Rangers. Chad was a line-drive-hitting, base hit-collecting machine when we were teammates. Conversely, I couldn't buy a hit. But he had something I didn't…he had a clear mind, a vision and a goal. I had worry, doubt and frustration. In professional baseball, no performance quickly leads to no job.

When I was released in the spring of 1991, I started giving batting lessons and helping young hitters. I always had a good feel for the swing and how to teach it, but back then I was focused exclusively on the mechanics of hitting and never the mental art of hitting. I finished my degree in Physical Education from Dallas Baptist University and took a job as a physical education teacher and baseball coach in Forney, Texas. We had a ton of success with our baseball team because of hard-working young men who loved to play, but our main goal was to out-work everyone we played.

When it comes to hitting a baseball, practically everyone has their two cents worth of knowledge. And you can go to any Little League park in America, and every coach and almost every fan believes they are a hitting coach. There have been many books written about hitting or how to go about teaching someone to hit. I have read many of those books and studied many so-called "hitting authorities," and the theme almost always seems to be focused on the feel of the swing, mastering the bat path toward the ball and many other mechanics. All those mechanical things are important. Just as it is vitally important that the engine of a vehicle is mechanically sound.

Think about this: If your engine is mechanically sound, your car is a vehicle that can take you where you want to go. But it will not take you where you want to go simply because it is mechanically sound. You, as the driver, must have a plan. You must have the confidence that you can reach your desired destination. And you need to check often that you are on the right course. If you simply step into a mechanically sound car from a driveway in Dallas and decide to drive to someone else's driveway in Houston with no plan, no roadmap and no clue as to how to make sure you are on the right path, chances are you will never make it to Houston…or even out of Dallas.

That's an overly simplistic example, but the point is that to hit a baseball, we must to have a plan. Yes, we need to be mechanically solid, but we must understand that what we say in our head and how we say it will then allow our body to achieve it. It is the ability to be able to "connect the dots from our mind to our body that is so important. And it is vitally important to be able to internalize your goal of hitting a baseball consistently well before you will be successful externally. I don't just want you to be a hitter, I want you to internalize the thoughts of being an effective hitter, an exceptional hitter, a productive hitter. Let's set our goals accordingly and work to make them come true. The mental approach to hitting is even more important than being mechanically sound.

In this book we will examine the hitting disciplines and work to understand and control them, from the mental to the mechanical and then the physiological. My goal is to supply you with the mental and physical strategies to be a great hitter. I wish I had known these techniques many years ago, because I might have reached my dream destination. But I can't go back in time.

What I can do is provide you with the game plan to be a great hitter. I was inspired to write this book years ago after a 12-year-old named Seth Metzger mentioned it to me during a lesson one off-season at an academy in Plano, Texas. I then became motivated after the 2015 season because I felt like it was time to pass along the knowledge that could have been so beneficial to me as a player. I have poured my heart and soul into this book for the sole purpose of giving you ideas and thoughts that will help in your journey as a person, teammate, friend and hitter. With that said, I wish you the best in your endeavors. Now, let's turn the page in this book…and begin a new chapter in your baseball career.

PART 1

"We have to learn to be our own best friends because we fall too easily into the trap of being our own worst enemies."

– Roderick Thorp, Rainbow Drive

"No one can make you feel inferior without your consent."

– Eleanor Roosevelt

"Confidence is preparation. Everything else is beyond your control."

– Richard Kline

"If you are going to doubt something, doubt your limits."

– Don Ward

Chapter 1

The Voice Inside Our Head

Just for a moment, I would like you to think about a person who has had a powerfully positive impact on your life. Perhaps it was a parent, a grandparent, a coach, a teacher, a friend or some other sort of associate. What was it that made that person have such positive affect on you?

Obviously, I don't know your particular situation, but I am going to take an educated guess here. Even though I don't know you and I don't know the person who played such a powerful role in your life, either, my suspicion is that the person who came to mind spoke to you in a manner that gave you confidence and made you feel good about yourself and your abilities. Perhaps his/her words were assuring, filling you with optimism, courage, buoyancy, enthusiasm and belief. Whatever the case, that person intentionally invested in you in the hope that you would reach your goals and be successful. That person has been a true blessing in your life with his/her words of encouragement, and I am sure you are grateful for that powerful influence.

Here's the truth, though: No matter how positive that person's words were to you, they pale in comparison to the importance of your own words that you tell yourself. Make sure you understand this: Your confidence is the product of your thoughts...on the baseball diamond and in any other endeavor in life. In the mathematical equation of baseball and life, you need to remember this formula: Add to your self-worth and maximize your results by multiplying the positive affirmations you tell yourself. Conversely, you will subtract from your potential and minimize your results by multiplying your insecurities.

If you doubt yourself, then indeed you stand on shaky ground.
—Henrik Ibsen

The little voice inside your head will go further toward determining your success or failure as a hitter than any coach, any drill or any routine ever could. To this day, people poke fun of the late Yogi Berra's quote that states, "Baseball is 90 percent mental and the other half is physical." Yogi-isms are still good for a chuckle, but his point was essentially the same as Ty Cobb, who produced a career .366 batting average over the course of 24 seasons from 1905-28. Cobb once said, "What's above the [player's] shoulders is more important than what's below."

Think about that. Whatever is happening in your head is far more important than *anything* that is happening in the physical realm—your swing path, your mechanics, your hands, your hips, your entire lower half, your equipment and even your raw physical abilities. In the words of Henry Ford—not a baseball player, I realize, but an icon in American history—"If you think you can do a thing or think you can't do a thing, you're right." But here's the problem I see with so many baseball players at every level of the game: When something goes wrong, when your batting average dips, when you are mired in a slump, when the whole outfield looks like a big leather glove that is going to catch everything you hit, what is the tendency? For most players, it's to work on the physical mechanics of the game, to hit off a tee, to take lessons, to hit batting practice, etc. While there is absolutely nothing wrong with doing any of those things, if baseball is truly a mental game and mental preparation is the key, why are you spending all your time on addressing the less important element of the game? Wouldn't it be more beneficial to first begin addressing your mental preparation, you mental approach and mindset during every pitch?

So, here's my question to you: "Do you tell yourself good, productive things about your abilities? Do you say positive things even when your results are negative? Or do you beat yourself up and create doubt about what you can do?"

It is important to understand that you have a choice. You CAN become your own greatest coach and most powerful influence in your playing career and your life by simply adopting a positive outlook where you consistently build yourself up and encourage yourself to be great. Repeat after me: "I am great at what I do. I do a solid job of staying focused and staying in the moment. I commit to a thought, and I see it through. I have decided heart, which means my destiny is assured. I was made to succeed."

The flip side of those affirmations are negative emotions and knee-jerk reactions, which are—unfortunately—much more natural for most of us to feel and say to ourselves. For example: "Why can't I get better? Why can't I get over the hump and out of this slump? I can't focus on this pitch because I am reliving my last strikeout." Whether you know it or not, your mind is going all the time, and without realizing it, we sometimes fall into a negative mentality and expect negative results. But you can stop all the negative chatter and transform your thoughts into powerful and positive machine that will assure you a much brighter future. We simply must make a conscious effort to speak words of encouragement. WE HAVE THE CHOICE! YOU HAVE THE CHOICE! Your destiny is not in your hands. It's in your mind.

The first key is to identify the words you are using, and you must make a commitment to replace words and phrases like, "I can't, I don't, I have to" with words and phrases like "I will, I can, I have the strength." When you use ultimatum words—"I HAVE TO"—it typically makes you react in tense and stressful ways. To succeed at the plate, you need a steady heartbeat. You need to be calm and relaxed. Use powerful words that allow you to be more natural and fluid in your demeanor and actions.

Many hitters in the middle of a slump use phrases—internally and/or outwardly—like "I suck," "I am never getting out of this" or "it's hopeless." Anyone who has played this game for any length of time has been there and thought such defeating, pessimistic thoughts. It's easy to allow those thoughts because your results are not matching your expectations. But a huge step in the right direction is resisting that temptation. Even if you are only whispering those things to yourself or mulling them over in your mind, you are minimizing your potential and reducing your chance to succeed. Many books, self-help programs and seminars have been produced regarding the "law of attraction." Without going into great depths to explain what that means, the law of attraction means that 'like attracts like.' In other words, whether we realize it or not, we are responsible for bringing both positive and negative influences into our lives. According to the law of attraction, where you place your focus can have an intense impact on what happens to you because your unconscious mind doesn't decipher between reality and imagination. If you go to a fiction movie and are stirred to tears or moved by your fears, your conscious mind knows this is not reality. But your unconscious mind causes you to react in sadness, shock or in any other manner. Your unconscious mind is amazingly powerful, and if you spend your days telling yourself that you will never get a hit or that you suck as a hitter, your unconscious mind will take that as a fact, which will certainly affect your results.

Conversely, if you look for the silver lining in every experience, every at-bat and every opportunity, you will begin to sense positivity surrounding you every day. A huge step toward improving your outcome is to commit to saying things—even in the midst of struggles—that encourage your subconscious mind. For example, "I have unlimited potential, I am a great hitter, I am capable of getting back on track, I can fix anything in my swing."

Many times when a hitter struggles, the first thing he or his coaches address is a mechanical fix. That could be an issue, but if you can make a habit of improving your positive thought process, you will often discover that the flaw was more in your thinking than your actual swing. Please understand that your mental state is a direct connection to your mechanics. A good question to ask yourself is this: "Does the way I am thinking affect the mechanics of my swing?"

You undoubtedly know the answer. The way you talk to yourself absolutely affects your swing. When you take a proactive approach to your voice, you can begin by saying "I can do this" or "it's just a matter of time before I begin a hot streak." The reality is that you are only one swing or one thought away from being back in the groove.

When you chase hits, you drive yourself crazy because you are trying to force the issue, and the outcome is basically dictating your emotions and peace of mind. It's a constant struggle. As difficult as it is, you must redirect your perspective and approach, directing your thoughts toward controlling the only things you can control: your own private little voice. You can push the reset button and begin again by approaching your struggle with a thought like this: "Today, I am going to commit to being as relaxed and loose as I can be. I am just going to work on hitting low, line drives. Nothing else matters."

Those three words—nothing else matters—have a powerful way of focusing your full attention on the task at hand and the actual process that will get you back to your normal, natural self. It gives you a clearer and a more attainable goal. It keeps you focused on one thing, one thought and one goal, which is certainly more powerful and positive than being consumed by the pursuit of a "base hit." When you put pressure on yourself to deliver at the plate, it's easy to become tense, tight and stressed. You quit breathing naturally and become more robotic and slower.

It is extremely difficult—almost impossible—to think of more than one thing at a time. Your mind can easily wander from one thought to another, but it's practically impossible to focus on two things at once. As your mind wanders, that little voice inside your head increases in speed. When our voice is fast, our body is tense, which produces a slow, robotic swing. Fast thinking leads to a faster heartbeat, which produces tension and tightness that slow you down. Committing to one thought, however, slows everything down. We can challenge ourselves to focus on one thought for as little as five seconds at a time. That's approximately how long the sequence of a pitch lasts, so committing to one thought starts in the preparation of your daily routine, beginning in your spare time and then your batting cage work. With no pressure to produce a base hit, it all starts by focusing on one thing for five seconds. One swing at a time and one thought at a time doesn't seem so difficult, does it?

The Voice Inside Our Head

In working with hitters who are in different stages during the course of the season, I always find it rather amazing to hear some of the things those players tell me. With the hitter who is struggling, I usually hear something like, "I feel good in the cages and in batting practice, BUT I can't seem to find it in the game."

News flash: The game is when it counts! I've seen plenty of great "five o'clock hitters," but when the lights come on and the fans fill the stands for a seven o'clock game, that's when it matters. We know that, and when we are struggling, it's tempting to overwork physically because we have often been told that the harder we work, the more we are owed success. If we work hard and sweat, then it will pay off with base hits, right?

Wrong. Unfortunately, IT DOESN'T WORK THAT WAY! You can hit in the cage until your hands are a blistered mess. Your swing can feel perfect in practice, but if there is no mental commitment or no mental calmness, then the chances of success are limited, at best. The cold, hard truth is that the game doesn't owe you or me anything, and we can't master it by simply working hard and investing sweat equity. You won't have success because you are a good person or because you do the right things in practice. Having great mechanics is good, but it won't give you the results you want until you are in tune with the voice inside your head and at peace with your mental approach so that you can be in complete control during the crucial time: GAME TIME!

How can you control or change your thought?

When you start the process of changing your thought as a hitter, it's important to be committed to the thought you want in your head and to repeat it as you go through the routines of the day and into your individual work. Repeat your thought over and over, and work to say it slowly and methodically. Begin this habit tomorrow morning and work on repeating it throughout the day, as you brush your teeth, as you shower, as you eat breakfast and so forth. Start with something like, "Relax, relax, relax, relax, relax." Or: "Breathe, breathe, breathe, breathe, breathe." On the way to the ballpark, remind yourself one thing: "Be on time, be on time, be on time, be on time, be on time." In the clubhouse, the batting cage or the dugout, remind yourself: "Work down through the ball, work down through the ball, work down through the ball, work down through the ball, work down through the ball." Remember, the slower you talk to yourself, the more relaxed your body becomes and the more natural you feel.

If you have ever had a song in the morning that sticks with you, you know that you can spend the rest of the day humming it, whether you like the song or not. That's how your mind works with memorization. Begin chanting your thought for the moment in your internal voice, and the thought will stick with you for as long as you keep repeating it. The whole idea is to repeat what you want to repeat and to be diligent and focused on it. The more you say it, the better chance you have of memorizing it, making it part of your subconscious mind and executing it with your body.

Another good way to think about it is that your voice is like a computer. It's the hard drive. When the hard drive is given a command, the monitor, which serves as our body, then executes it.

Have you ever noticed hitters between pitches as they look to the third base coach for signs? As the sequence of signs is given, the hitter then goes back to preparing to

The Voice Inside Our Head

step back into the box. Many times you will see hitters adjust their batting gloves, tap their spikes with the bat or even take practice swings. Each hitter has his own unique routine that he goes through as he is in the at-bat. Most of the time, the hitter is not even aware of his exact mannerisms. He is deep in his own mind with his inner voice. He is either confident and locked-in or he is doubting himself, wondering why he just doesn't feel right. It's a constant battle all hitters must face. You have to ask yourself if you are committed to your one thought or are you telling yourself negative things?

It is important to focus on one thought five seconds at a time, because there are so many things that can come to mind at the plate, from wondering if the pitcher is going to pitch inside or outside, fastball or breaking ball, to thinking about your last at-bat, your batting average, etc. My suggestion is to focus on what you need to do to swing the way you want to swing. Feel good about yourself and your swing. It's when your thoughts are racing and you don't feel good about yourself that you are prone to try too hard or to do too much. Then you start lunging, opening up, etc. Find the one thought that will eliminate any clutter in your mind. Sometimes that seems impossible to do, but you can do it for five seconds. Focus on one thing for this one pitch! Just this pitch.

Thinking about the direction you want to hit the ball can also tighten up your swing. If you are lunging forward, you can work to hit down through the ball toward the middle of the field. Or you can focus on working your back hip to the ball through the middle of the field. If you are opening up, you can commit to hitting the ball to the opposite-field gap. If you feel late with your timing, focus on starting your timing off the pitcher's break of the hands.

Those are simple approach thoughts that can help without having to go through the grind of your mechanics. It is a major mistake to begin tinkering with your mechanics or thinking about correcting mechanics in the middle of a game or the middle of an at-bat. Instead, commit to one thought and repeat it in your head over and over. You have the choice. You have the ability. It is in your complete control!

The reply I often hear to those statements is: "Well, I am trying." Stop trying! There is no trying in hitting; you either swing or you don't. You either make contact or you don't. You either get a hit or you don't. You are either in control or you are not. Commit to a thought or don't. Get the picture? When you find yourself back to feeling right with your swing, then your focus or your thought can be shifted to thinking along with the pitcher…if that is part of your game plan. You have the choice to either commit to the thought of your swing, the thought of your direction or the thought of sitting on a pitch. But you can't do it all and produce the results you want.

"You and I are not what we eat; we are what we think."

— *Walter Anderson*

"The world we have created is a product of our thinking; it cannot be changed without changing our thinking."

— *Albert Einstein*

"Thoughts are like an open ocean. They can either move you forward within its waves, or sink you under deep into its abyss."

— *Anthony Liccione*

Chapter 2

Matching up a thought with a feeling

Your mind is the most powerful thing God gave you, because what you can conceive, you can achieve. Your mind controls your body's actions, as well as your attitude and outlook. As you strive to become a better hitter, you must understand that in order to make adjustments, you must first make the mental decision to improve. Think about that. Improvement doesn't just happen. Becoming better requires that you make the decision to improve. If your mind is committed to improving—really committed and convinced that you are on the verge of major breakthroughs—your body will follow suit.

Conceive, believe and achieve!

Please understand that you can never be perfect with your swing. As I've noted, failure is a major part of this game, and if you are committed to always improving—as opposed to reaching the impossible destination of perfection—you will be better equipped to make adjustments and to move forward. Because of the amount of failure in baseball, even the best hitters to ever play the game need to continually make adjustments.

Many times, though, hitters are fearful of improvement because of the possibility of somehow losing the swing, the muscle memory or the positive habits they already possess. Fear is typically a huge issue with hitters who are struggling to move beyond a slump.

Matching up a thought with a feeling

Depending on the level of the game, a struggling hitter is often dealing with fear of failure, losing a job, not playing, disappointing someone, being released, not making the team, etc. Those things worry and weigh upon us, and we often spend many hours thinking about fear. But if fear is our focus, how can we ever expect to improve? On the other hand, if improvement is what we constantly think about. It's just a matter of time before that becomes our reality.

One of the practices that has often helped me overcome my fears, as well as many of the players I've worked with, is to play the mental game that I call "what's the worst that can happen?" Think about that from a hitter's perspective: What's the worst thing that can happen when you step into the batter's box?

Obviously, you could make an out. You could fail to improve. You could lose the confidence of your manager or coach. You could be benched, demoted, released and so forth. While none of those things are particularly pleasant thoughts, they don't represent the end of the world, either. Making an out is simply part of the game. And if sitting on the bench or being released from a team forces you to make the necessary adjustments to improve your swing, then those things could be a blessing.

The point is that if we really examine our fears, it will often become obvious that, in the historic words of the late President Franklin D. Roosevelt, "the only thing we have to fear…is fear itself."

As a hitter, you need to focus on what you can control. You can't control the speed or location of the pitch or the skill level of the pitcher. You can't control the alignment of the defense; the direction of the wind; the depth of the outfield fences; the strategy utilized by the opposing manager/coach;

the range of the middle infielders; or many other factors that may eventually factor into whether or not you end up on base.

What you can control is your mind. You can also maintain the discipline and desire to improve, and you can stay committed to evolving as a player, learning each day and believing that you can accomplish whatever you set your mind to do. Identify your motivation, and let it drive you to reach the goals you have set for yourself.

Now, back to the realization that perfection is impossible in hitting, but there is always room for improvement. Consider this: No Major League hitter—not even the greatest of the greats—has ever hit 1.000 or even .500. for an entire season. In fact, no one has hit .400 in a season since the legendary Ted Williams hit .406 in 1941.

All styles of hitters have had success, and all styles of hitters will continue to have success. Hitters with high leg kicks and players with no stride have succeeded at every level. Styles and techniques come and go, but the common traits for every successful hitter are confidence and trust. We are all wired differently. What makes one person tick may not work for the next person…and vice versa. That's why it is extremely important to spend time with yourself and to discover what style works best for you.

With that said, though, we can all take a similar approach in terms of understanding that a thought will lead to an action. When you are working to improve your swing in a certain area, seek to find a powerful word that you can tie to the desired move. For example, if you are working to shorten your swing, you first need to understand how you are going to accomplish it. Are you swinging too hard? Are you attempting to do too much? Is your bat path working too much uphill? Are you losing your balance?

Swinging too hard or trying to do too much can be altered by applying conscious thought into the amount of effort being exerted. If you are swinging at 95 percent of your capacity, back off and work on your swing at about 60 to 70 percent. If your bat path is too much uphill, work to hit down through the ball more. If you are losing your balance, then swing and hold your finish for at least five seconds.

Now as you swing, repeat in your head in a chanting voice, 70 percent, 70 percent, 70 percent. You can even chant "smooth and easy." If you are swinging uphill then chant, "work down through ball." You can also chant something as simple as "short to the ball." Give power to your thought and say it as you are swinging and repeat it.

It is empowering to say that each and every issue with your swing can be improved. As you work to improve, you will learn to have a way to simplify your thought process and learn to channel the voice in your head to one thought.

Our daily preparation (thoughts away from the field)

When you are feeling good and are having success at the plate, good feelings and good thoughts consume your mind. In those times, issues with your swing are far from your mind. You are just feeling great, and you can't wait to arrive at the ballpark, regardless of who is pitching.

When you are in a bit of a funk, however, your mind is consumed by what is wrong. How can you fix it? Is it your timing? Or your bat path? Are you waiting on the ball, are you leaking forward? In the midst of a slump, however, hitters often spend countless hours dissecting and searching for answers. But the most disturbing and disruptive thing many hitters do is replaying the bad swings and bad at-bats in their minds. They go to bed replaying a rollover or a popup with the bases loaded. They focus on failures as opposed to just failing in one instance.

Then they wake up in the morning and go right back to those at-bats and come to the conclusion that they are in a slump. Then questions or comments come from friends or family: *What's wrong with you? You are really struggling.*

The challenge is to remind yourself of this: When things are going good, you are thinking strong, positive and assertive thoughts. You are feeling good! Baseball is so much easier and more enjoyable when you feel that way about yourself. So, why not make it easier on yourself in the midst of a slump to remind yourself to feel good about yourself and to think strong, positive and assertive thoughts?

Sometimes, it may not be that simple, but you we struggle as a hitter, the problem or issue is usually always minor. The mechanics of your good swing when we you are hitting really well isn't lost from one day to the next. It is usually your thought process that changes, and you misinterpret it to be mechanical issues.

When you remind yourself of the thoughts you are feeling when you are in a rhythm at the plate, you are utilizing a mental discipline to repeat those good thoughts. Remember that positive thoughts lead to positive results. Go to bed visualizing your good swings and good at-bats, regardless of what your results might have been the last week. Wake up with your good swings in mind.

The mind does not know the difference between real and imagination. Therefore, you have the ability to trick your mind right back into your good swings. A good example is visualizing eating your favorite dessert. If you think about it long enough then your mouth will start to salivate and your craving will become stronger.

Another good practice would be to start your preparation when you wake up. After breakfast and a shower, spend a few minutes studying the opposing pitcher and bullpen you will be facing. Watch video of the opposing starter and watch hitters who are similar to you against the particular pitcher. Watch how the pitcher attacks hitters, what types of pitches he throws in different counts and make a mental note of his out pitch. Formulate your game plan before the rest of your morning routine. Then go to park and prepare your swing and approach. I suggest this routine because I happen to know a successful big leaguer who does that every day.

Younger hitters may not have the luxury of all the videos or statistics, but to be successful, prepare for every contest. Whether you visualize yourself having solid at-bats or visualize the mechanics of the opposing pitcher, be ready and committed to your game plan and to thinking in a positive manner.

Life is really simple, but we insist on making it complicated.

— Confucius

Baseball statistics are like a girl in a bikini. They show a lot, but not everything.

— Toby Harrah

Life is amazingly good when it's simple and amazingly simple when it's good.

— Terri Guillemets

Chapter 3
Learning to Hit the Reset Button

Technology is a wonderful thing...when it works. When they are not working properly, however, technological devices can be quite aggravating. After all, many of us rely heavily on our smart phones, laptops, tablets and so forth. When they are not functioning, our productivity can come screeching to a halt.

The good news is that the solution to our technological problems are often an easy one. Simply turning off your laptop, smart phone or tablet and restarting it will often solve all that ails the device. Even malfunctioning computer components in vehicles can often be fixed by simply stopping the vehicle, turning off the engine and then restarting it. Rebooting a device is often the key to restoration.

Here's even better news: It works for your mind, as well. You must always remember that your thoughts lead to actions. If you know yourself and how your mind works, it will allow you to reboot and to find solutions much faster than your peers who are not familiar with the mental reset button.

As a baseball player, you need a reset button when you do not feel as good as you should about your swing. You need something that gives you hope and confidence to realize that you are not a lost cause. Sometimes, a good night's sleep is the reset button you need. But many times the reset button is simply a thought that will help you eliminate worries about mechanics, statistics or results. It could be something as simple as a "swing key" or thinking about hitting the ball in a certain direction. It could be many things, but it needs to be something to take your mind off of negative results and to give you peace of mind.

I personally recall a left-handed hitter who was going through a dry spell and couldn't reclaim the consistency he desired at the plate. This question was posed to him: "What do you do when you are going good and locked in at the plate?"

Without hesitation, he said: "I work to hit a line drive over the shortstop's head into the left centerfield gap. I can get that hit 40 percent of my at-bats." This follow-up question was then asked: "What percentage of the time do you have quality at-bats when you work to hit a line drive over the shortstop's head?"

By his own estimation, he concluded that when he focused on going the opposite way and hitting a line drive over the shortstop's head, he had quality at-bats 70 percent of the time. He then realized that the simplest solution to his struggles was to focus on that thought. Forget about mechanics. Forget about the last game. Forget about everything…except for hitting the ball on a line over the shortstop's head.

Sounds too simple to be true, right? But the reality is that sometimes the simple solution is the best. You don't need to be a computer specialist or technological genius to restart your laptop or your Wi-Fi modem. You just need to realize that, from time to time, the key to productivity is a refreshing reboot. The message you send your mind is just as powerfully refreshing. In the midst of struggling at the plate, you often can't see the forest for the trees. That's when you need to go back to something that has worked for you in the past and make it a simple, but powerful thought.

Conversely, be aware of what you are doing during those times you are locked in and hitting everything on the button. Remember the power of humility and gratitude when everything is falling for a hit or just outside of the infielder's reach. Be thankful for your good times and keep things in perspective because the ego has a way of wrecking our good runs. There is a big difference between inner confidence and visual arrogance.

Failure to stay grounded in good times often leads to becoming greedy. Instead of staying focused on the little things that have contributed to your success (like going the other way and hitting line drives into the gap), you start trying to do a little more, to hit it farther and to do more damage, swinging for the fences instead of the gaps. When you start down that road, over-swings lead to pop-ups or ground outs on pitches down the heart of the plate. Before you know it, you start thinking that something may be wrong with your swing. You can't understand why you missed such a fat pitch. You start the search for the issue and go down the checklist, looking for things that aren't even there. Stay humble during the good stretches and avoid the temptation to do too much.

I've seen many times when a hitter has been locked in for a while and feels great. In a game where he is having success and the team is rolling, he comes to the plate and decides he is going to let it rip and ends up popping out. Perhaps he receives one more at-bat late in the game and he grounds out. The team won the game and he contributed, but he can't help but to wonder about what happened on those last two at-bats. He goes home feeling good, but he can't remove the last two swings from his mind. Uncertainty settles in, and a slump is soon to follow, as he searches for mechanical issues that made him fail. In reality, the issue was caused by the ego. He tried to do too much. Period.

What the hitter needs is not a fat pitch, time with his personal hitting instructor or to dissect his swing mechanics on slow-motion video; he needs to hit the reset button. That sounds so simple, but remember that the simple solution is often the best. One other note to remember when searching for swing solutions: Video can be a great tool for you, but as sports psychologist Dr. Bob Rotella has stated: "A hitter should never watch video of himself when he knows darn well that his mind was not in a good place." Makes total sense. Don't watch video searching for an answer without remembering your state of mind and what you were thinking during the at-bat. If your thinking was flawed, reboot and refresh.

The daily "in the moment" short term goals

The only way to climb a mountain is to take one step at a time. The only way to eat an elephant is one bite at a time. The journey of a 1,000 miles begins with a single step. And to finish reading this book, you must start be reading the words that comprise each page of each chapter. So many things in life are accomplished by a specific, rudimentary process. Writing a book can seem overwhelming at first, but not if you break it down into chapters, paragraphs and sentences. You string together sentences, you create a paragraph. You put paragraphs together, you have a chapters. And multiple chapters become a book. That's called breaking it down and staying in the moment.

Baseball players do not always do that. Many times as a hitter, you want to look at the hits and the statistics at the end of the year and try to speed up the process. But let's face it: Anything worth doing will take time, and if you want to make the most of the experience, you must be aware of each step along the way. No matter how hard you try, you cannot hit a six-run homer collect three hits in your final at-bat of the game to make up for the poor at-bats early in the contest. The only way to have success is to stay in control every pitch of every at-bat. You never want to try to do too much, and you always want to value every pitch. Staying focused on every pitch of every at-bat is probably one of the most difficult things to do in baseball.

It's so easy and tempting to look ahead, especially when things aren't going as well as you would like them. Hitters also stay in the past too long because we are either searching for answers to failed at-bats or reliving the great at-bats. The problem is that when your thoughts are in either the past or the future, you often create anxiety and stress in the present. When you stay in the present, you are more engaged and can be more focused on the now. The only way to recognize a pitch to hit is to be focused on the pitch so you can make a good decision to put a good swing at it.

Your focus on trying to get a hit places the cart before the horse. You are skipping an important part of the process, which tends to make a hitter over-aggressive and leads to swinging at bad pitches or getting yourself out. Sometimes, you can talk yourself into swinging before a pitch is even thrown, which leads to swinging at balls out of the zone. This tends to happen when you are in a good hitters count like 1-0, 2-0, 3-1 or 3-0. If you are focused in on every pitch of the at-bat, however, you have a better chance of catching yourself from over doing it.

A very powerful step is to define achievable goals on a daily basis. It all can start before you arrive at the park. Instead of shooting for outcome goals, you can start by having a simple goal of having fun and relaxing. As the pregame preparations begin, you can strive to set short-term goals, transitioning from cage work to batting practice and then formulate your game plan for that contest. Before each and every swing in prep work, state to yourself that you are going to:

- You are going to stay on top of the ball
- You are going to maintain your balance
- You are going to swing smoothly
- You are going to hit low line drives

This process can be for just three swings and then you may take a short break. Assess how you fared for three swings. Were you committed to one thought for three swings? If so, you can work to accomplish it for five swings. Take a break and assess. Setting your goals is totally dependent on your ability to stay committed to the one thought, the one thing that you are working to improve. The thought can change, but there needs to be a 100 percent commitment each and every swing. The whole idea is to repeat the thought and the feeling one swing at a time. That—and that alone—is the short-term goal.

Batting practice can be beneficial if your goals are set accordingly. It can also have a negative affect and make you frustrated if you set unattainable goals or you don't have a solid thought that you are working to execute. It is also important to remember that your practice doesn't always determine your game performance. Also, one swing or one thought—if not executed—does not define who and what you are. Work to repeat the good thoughts and the good swings. Feel it and repeat it. PLEASE NOTE: It's not feel it and then try to do it better and bigger. Be content with doing it well and not trying to hit for the cycle in one plate appearance.

I learned from one player as he was working out one winter that his goal every time he worked on his swing was to have a boring swing. What does that mean? To him, it meant that it was the same swing time after time after time. You want to repeat the same swing, thought, effort, balanced finish and direction. Ask yourself this: Is your swing boring or exciting? A boring swing is one that you can repeat over and over.

This thought came from an MLB catcher who would take every swing and try to repeat it. His thought process, effort and mechanics were similar every time. His idea was to groove his swing over and over. He wanted to hit the ball in the same area over and over again. This can be a good challenge for all of us. Next time you go hit, bore yourself.

Keep striving to reach your short-term goals, which may be as simple as going back to "just this pitch" or "just this thought" or "just this swing."

One cannot think crooked and walk straight.
> *—Author Unknown*

No problem can withstand the assault of sustained thinking.
> *—Voltaire*

Success comes in cans, not cant's.
> *—Author Unknown*

Chapter 4
The power of "ONE"

Motivational speaker and successful author Brian Tracy says that you have complete control over only one thing in the universe: your thinking. In any situation, you can decide what you are going to think. Your thoughts and the way you interpret any event trigger your feelings—positive or negative. Your thoughts and feelings lead to your actions and determine the results you achieve. But it all starts with your thoughts. Furthermore, Tracy writes: "The Law of Substitution says, 'Your mind can hold only one thought at a time, positive or negative. You can substitute a positive thought for a negative thought whenever you choose.' You can apply this law by deliberately thinking about something positive whenever you want to cancel out a thought or feeling that makes you angry or unhappy."

This is a key point remember in your career as a baseball player, as well as your overall development as a person. Let this sink in: Your mind can only hold one thought at a time. As such, the power of "ONE" is extraordinary. As a hitter, you can only be successful if you focus on one thought, one idea, one task, one pitch, one swing, one phrase, one hit, or one at-bat at a time. Understanding this simple concept can allow you to free your mind from clutter and to develop your approach at the plate, your approach at practice and your overall ability to stay in the moment.

When all else fails, train yourself to think of one thought or phrase so you can concentrate on one pitch or one swing. The power of ONE is literally what mental discipline is all about because it allows you to block out everything else and to concentrate on just one thing at a time.

What can I do to help me with my thought discipline?

Like your body requires daily nutrition, the voice in your head needs daily attention. Quite frankly, that voice is so much more important than anyone else's in terms of how you talk to yourself. Brian Tracy, in his book *Change Your Thinking, Change Your Life*, wrote: "The most powerful words in your vocabulary are the words that you say to yourself and believe. Your self-talk, your inner dialogue, determines 95 percent of your emotions. When you talk to yourself, your subconscious mind accepts these words as commands. It then adjusts your behavior, your self-image and your body language to fit a pattern consistent with those words."

In other words, our inner voice defines who you are and how you think about yourself. And how you think about yourself holds the key to how you are viewed by others. Consequently, one of the most powerful things you can possibly say to yourself is: "I like myself and I love my life." Or, "I am a man of character and integrity." Or, "I am a great hitter and I love this game."

Whatever words you repeatedly tell yourself becomes part of your subconscious mind. Your parents, coaches and teachers could be constantly building you up with positive affirmations, but if your inner voice is telling you that you're a failure, a loser, a bad hitter or anything else along those lines, you will fail. Conversely, your parents, coaches, teachers and so forth could verbally abuse and belittle you, but as long as your inner voice continues to build yourself up, you will succeed. The reality is that your inner voice is with you at every moment of your life. It's the most powerful voice in your world. Obviously, the best-case scenario is when you have positive people around you who are constantly building you up with the positive things that they say. But no one else has as much power to propel you as your own inner voice.

That voice is always looking for direction on what to say, how to say it and when to say something. It is a never-ending challenge to continually feed yourself with positive talk, but the more quickly you can make that a habit, the better off you will be. It's a great habit to begin your day each morning with positive affirmations. As soon as you step out of bed tomorrow morning, speak positively to yourself. Whether you are in the shower, getting dressed, driving to school or going through any other part of your daily routine, say these kinds of things to yourself:

- Today is a great day, and I will seize this day
- I like myself and I love my work habits
- I am made in the image of God, and I am bound for greatness
- I am a great hitter, and I love to play this game
- I am the best, I'm the best, I'm the best

Whatever food for thought you can give yourself will direct and strengthen you...as long as that food is positive. Don't feed yourself junk and then expect to be healthy and successful. Feed yourself wonderfully positive and uplifting words, and those words will become self-fulfilling prophecies. We just have to make our positive self-talk a matter of extreme importance. As you work to become a better version of yourself, it's extremely beneficial to utilize books and audio programs that will freshen your understanding of your individuality. Here are a few of my favorite books that can help in your journey:

- The Bible
- "What to Say When You Talk to Yourself" by Shad Helmstetter
- "The Power of Positive Thinking" by Norman Vincent Peale
- "Mindset: The New Psychology of Success" by Carol Dweck
- "All In: You Are One Decision Away From a Totally Different Life" by Mark Batterson
- "Develop the Mental Strength of a Warrior" by Gregg Swanson

The aforementioned books are just some of my favorites that will likely spark your desire to learn more about yourself and how your mind works. Reading those books and others like them will provide you with tools to make you a high achiever in anything. In this era of technology, I also think it is important to use your time wisely by listening to audio programs whenever possible. While it's true that leaders are readers, you can also listen to great books like the ones I mentioned or many others through your smart phone while traveling, working out, walking your dogs and so forth.

Feeding your mind with positive, educational and motivational material is a never-ending quest that can always be improved upon as you work to become the best you possible. You may take backward steps at times, but set your goals high and commit to working on you and to speaking positive thoughts to yourself.

It is also important to note that we, as hitters, will definitely learn more about ourselves through our failures than through our successes. Failing is a big part of life and baseball because it molds us into tough warriors. But no matter what you are going through, speak positively about yourself.

Practice what you preach, model of consistency

"We are what we repeatedly do. Excellence, therefore, is not an act but a habit."

– *Aristotle*

What a powerful quote. And it makes perfect sense. But if we acknowledge and accept that excellence is a result of our habits, why do we sometimes struggle with mediocrity?

The habit of our self-talk is why. We constantly need to encourage our inner voice. It's so easy to become frustrated with yourself and to speak negatively to yourself while walking back to the dugout following a strikeout or failing to move a runner to the next base. Most people curse themselves far more quickly than they would say something similar to another person.

But the best of the best in any field understand the importance of being your own cheerleader. In the midst of a slump, it's not easy or natural to remind yourself that you are the best and that you are destined for greatness. It's also not easy to remain relaxed and confident.

The natural tendency in a slump is to start second-guessing yourself or to begin seeking the advice of others. When you are in a tailspin and seek advice from others, everyone seems to have suggestions, although nothing seems to be working. Finally, you become so frustrated by the constant stress and grind that the voice in your head finally screams, "Stop it!" Or, "Screw it!" You finally tell yourself to stop pressing and to relax. That's when your real person shows up and says enough is enough. That's also when the hits start falling in once again. I've seen it a million times and been through it personally more times than I care to remember.

The thing you must realize is that the real person was there all the time. You just didn't look for him or work to rely on him. Instead of being your own cheerleader and focusing on one positive thought, it's so easy to seek the advice of others and to begin focusing on one suggestion after another. But the reality is that the quicker you can remind yourself to focus on one thing and to stay positive, the faster you will find a renewed sense of worth and confidence. We all choose our own thoughts, but we don't all choose them wisely. Choose to be upbeat; exercise mental discipline by refusing to say negative words to yourself; don't make excuses; don't feel sorry for yourself; and choose to remind yourself that you are the best.

When you channel it positively and effectively, your inner voice can be like a great coach, teacher or parent who brings out the best in you. Believe in yourself in all circumstances, and you will be amazed at the results you can achieve. But another critical point is to focus on what you want—good at-bats, a good swing, solid contact, line drives, etc.—and not what you don't want. So many people focus on what they don't want in life, like debt, disease, divorce and so forth. But as they focus on avoiding those things, they actually attract them. Focus on what you want—the positive things you want—like personal wealth, great health, happy relationships and so forth. As you focus and imagine those things clearly, you will attract them.

The same thing goes for your at-bats. Focus on envisioning line drives and the sound of the ball coming solidly off your at-bat. Spend time daily dreaming of the best scenarios and perfect outcomes. Remind yourself that you are the best. Write down your goals and your positive affirmations and review them once a day. But don't just read through them. Read through each goal, close your eyes and really try to feel the emotion of achieving that goal as if you had already accomplished it. Relive all the positive feelings and emotions of you at your best, and it will strengthen your focus, belief and confidence.

There is something magical that happens when you not only repeat positive affirmations to yourself, but you also write them down in the present tense. You will dramatically increase the power of your inner voice when you also include the power of the pen. Here are some other examples of power statements that will lead you to success (as you read them, truly believe them about yourself):

- I have a strong-willed mind
- I am always eager to improve
- I am a positive person, the glass is always half full
- I believe in my abilities and I am on the verge of greatness
- I am committed to my positives thoughts and my approach
- I am my own best motivator
- I accept challenges because they make me great.
- I am in control of my career
- I am in control of my work ethic
- I compete in any circumstance
- I am comfortable hitting with two strikes
- I am a line drive-producing machine
- I am the best

When you sit down to do this exercise, you must always be mindful of writing proactive, positive and powerful statements. In other words, focus on things such as, "I am a line-drive hitter" instead of "I don't hit pop-ups." Those two statements may seem like the same thing, but your subconscious mind takes over and begins to either create an image of a line drive into the gap or a pop-up. If I tell you not to think of chocolate-covered strawberries, what comes instantly to mind?

Chocolate-covered strawberries.

As we stated at the start of this chapter, you have complete control over only one thing in the universe: your thinking. So control it with positive affirmations, building yourself up and preparing yourself for greatness. The more you see yourself in a positive light, succeeding at the highest levels and achieving your dreams, the faster others will see you doing those things on the diamond or in any other walk of life.

Always be a first-rate version of yourself, instead of a second-rate version of somebody else.

– Judy Garland

Your time is limited, so don't waste it living someone else's life.

– Steve Jobs

The strongest force in the universe is a human being living consistently with his identity.

– Tony Robbins

Chapter 5
Know Thyself

From 2008-2011, it's a safe bet that just about every boy playing Little League baseball in the Dallas-Fort Worth area dreamed of being Josh Hamilton. In '08, Hamilton burst onto the Metroplex market and then made national news on July 14, 2008, when he clubbed 28 homers, a single-round record, in the first round of the Home Run Derby at Yankee Stadium. Hamilton didn't win the overall title, but he wowed the Yankee Stadium crowd and all those watching on national television. Two years later, he led the Texas Rangers to their first World Series in franchise history, when he was the 2010 American League MVP. He was also an All-Star in 2011, when he led the Rangers back to the World Series. During those four seasons, Hamilton was easily the most popular professional athlete in the Dallas-Fort Worth area, as he lifted majestic homers into the upper decks of stadiums across the country.

In Boston, there was a similar love affair for David Ortiz, although his star in Beantown burned brightly for much longer than Hamilton's did in Arlington. From the time he arrived in Boston in 2003 until his final glorious year with the Red Sox in 2016, "Big Papi" was a menacing, mashing home-run hitter with light tower power and a penchant for producing in the clutch. Ortiz was part of three World Series titles with the Red Sox, including 2013 when he was the World Series MVP. Ortiz, probably the most important Red Sox player since Ted Williams to the Boston faithful, was a fan favorite in Fenway for so many reasons, but the biggest reason was his ability to blast storybook homers.

Know Thyself

The story is also similar in Detroit, where young fans idolized Miguel Cabrera. In Washington, the youngsters love long-ball hitting Bryce Harper. In Chicago, the Cubs put an end to 108 years of curses in 2016 thanks in large part to the power-hitting duo of Kris Bryant and Anthony Rizzo. Mark McGwire and Sammy Sosa were there stars of the late 1990s because of their remarkable power numbers. And if you surveyed any group of baseball fans about the most influential player in the history of the game, chances are strong that Babe Ruth would be the player most often mentioned. The reason: Historic, mesmerizing, Hollywood-like home runs. Contrary to the famous line in the late-1990s Nike commercial, it's not just chicks who dig the long ball. Everybody in baseball loves the long ball, and every kid who picks up a bat envisions being a home run-hitting hero like Hamilton, Ortiz, McGwire, Sosa, Ruth, Barry Bonds, Albert Pujols, Reggie Jackson, Hank Aaron or so many other famous names in history.

Here's the problem, though: Those guys are genetic freaks of nature. The ball sounds different coming off of their bats because they are different than the rest of the players in the game and the rest of the humans on the planet. When average guys like me—and probably you—attempt to hit Ruthian dingers into the next stratosphere, it's a recipe for rollovers, groundouts, strikeouts and pop flies. The worst thing a contact, singles or line-drives hitter can do is to attempt to be something he is not. To thrive in this game—or even to survive—you must know who you are, who you are not and what kind of role you can play to stay in the game. In the words of former MLB player and manager Charlie Manuel, "Dang son, you got to know thyself! What kind of hitter are you?"

Most highlights on ESPN or MLB Network show power by way of the home run and the power arm. So, logically youngsters want to emulate the stars they see on television.

Power is a beautiful, wonderful thing, but it is something that shows up—if at all—as a result of many hours, days, weeks, months and years of working to become a hitter first. When young hitters typically search for power, there are a few things that are inevitably being sacrificed, such as the ability to make contact , proper balance, control, the ability to hit different pitches in different parts of the strike zone and tension, which is a direct connection to anxiety and frustration. A good question to ask anyone who is currently playing the game or played the game at one point in his life is, "How many times did you try to hit a home run and actually succeed at it? The likely answer is: Not very often.

Most of the time players succeed hitting for power when they are at their most relaxed state. That occurs when hitters are committed to a thought or to a particular game plan. The thought process is usually something along the lines of "finding a good pitch to hit," or "looking for something to drive." Many players who do hit with power are simply "looking for something out over the plate." In reality, there are three types of hitters:

- **Contact hitter**s: These are usually smaller players with quickness and speed, but not always. This type of hitter makes contact consistently. He has a knack for putting the barrel on the ball, placing the ball in play, getting on base and scoring runs.
- **Line drive hitters**: Most players fall in this category. This is a hitter who can hit line drives into the gaps and drives in runs. This type of hitter tends to produce plenty of doubles.
- **Power hitters**: These guys are usually the bigger framed players, but not always. When these guys connect, it produces a different sound and travels beyond the average hitters. On the down side, this

type of hitter tends to swing and miss more than the other two, but not always.

The ideal goal is to become a combination of all three types of hitters. Throughout history, guys like Rickey Henderson, Mike Schmidt, Ichiro Suzuki, Ken Griffey, Jr., Mike Trout, Mickey Mantle and Willie Mays, to name a few, have been a great combination of the three kinds of hitters. Obviously, not all players are gifted with power, so for most aspiring players the best goal is to be a contact and line drive hitter. To achieve that goal requires an all-consuming commitment in practices, thought processes and games.

All good hitters base their swing off the line drive. It is the one thing that never slumps. Ground balls and fly balls will be caught. Of course, line drives will be caught as well, but they spend less time in the air and increase your chances of reaching safely.

The question is: Can you make every swing a repeatable, line drive-producing swing? The answer: YES! It all starts with your tee work. Practice hitting line drives all the time. Not occasionally; not most of the time; all of the time. If you have the opportunity to hit in a cage, work on hitting line drives off the back net. When hitting in a cage, always try to hit the back of the net, not the sides of the net or the top of it. Your goal should be to repeat a line drive swing every time.

When you work off the back net, you are attempting to attack the ball in a similar fashion every time. You can move the tee inside or outside, but your objective should be to work off the back net. When you move the tee inside and tend to hit the side net, you are working around the ball. When you move the tee outside and are hitting the side net, you are cutting or slicing the ball. If you do either of these things, strive to feel when you are cutting the ball or working around the ball (hooking it). Another good practice is to avoid moving the tee way inside or way outside to the edges of the plate. When you move the tee big distances, you tend to make the plate bigger, which is why you may feel like you must reach to hit a ball outside or open to hit a ball inside. Again, the goal is to practice ONE swing and work to master it.

For those hitters who have power, it's still wise to work on becoming a solid line drive hitter first. If you can achieve that, the power, which is always there, shows up more consistently. It's a beautiful thing to be a great contact hitter who hits line drives and hits for power, as well. It's the best of all worlds, and it is possible. After all, nothing is impossible.

As you work to become the best combination hitter you can be, it is healthy to be accountable to yourself and to perform a daily assessment of your preparation and performance. You need to always start with the positives and the good things about your game. Then you can identify the limitations. Once you do that, you have a better sense of how to game plan and to set your daily short term goals. If you do this, you are being proactive in your daily approach. Make this part of your daily routine, and you will evolve into a much better hitter.

When you acknowledge your strengths, as well as your limitations, you are able to best develop your role. For example, if one of your strengths is hitting pitches on the inner half of the plate, but you lack consistency on pitches middle to the outer half, you must first remember to continue to maintain your strength (inner half) and game plan how to improve hitting the outer half. When you are proactive, you begin a habit of thinking that there are solutions to any problem you face. You become more of a growth-minded individual as opposed to a fix-minded one as described by author Caroline Dweck in the book, "*Mindset.*"

A growth-minded person believes he can always improve and evolve. He creates the belief that he can find answers to problems. A fix-minded person, on the other hand, sees things as they are. It is what it is. He just deals with it. While it is good to deal with it, why not take it and take it a step further and game plan to make it better?

As a hitter, you will encounter many different thoughts and ideas when it comes to hitting. As you are coached, you should always remember that people are trying to help you become better. So when advice is given, remember it is either going to help you apply it to your swing or it is something that does not apply to you. You must decide. Usually the simpler it is to understand, the better suited it can be for you.

When you strongly desire to improve, you will be more apt to study, read and learn as much as you can to apply things that will help give you an edge. It is a healthy task to study and find role models in the Major Leagues who are comparable to you in stature, style and look. You can study to find information about those players, where they grew up, where they went to school, what motivates them, what helped them succeed and so forth. You don't have to mimic everything about those players, but if you are 5-foot-9 and 175 pounds, it's good to find similar-sized players to study. If you are built like Dustin Pedroia (5-foot-8), Adam Eaton (5-foot-8) or Andrew McCutchen (5-10) don't try to swing like David Ortiz, Miguel Cabrera or Pablo Sandoval. Know who you are.

"For as he thinketh in his heart, so is he: Eat and drink, saith he to thee; but his heart is not with thee."
Proverbs 23:7 (KJV)

"Slump? I ain't in no slump… I just ain't hitting."
— Yogi Berra

Baseball is the only field of endeavor where a man can succeed three times out of ten and be considered a good performer.

— Ted Williams

Chapter 6
Hold that thought…for five seconds

Contrary to the perception of some moviegoers and casual baseball fans, sabermetrics and rigorous statistical analysis of non-conventional baseball statistics didn't begin with the release of *"Moneyball"*—the 2003 book written by Michael Lewis or the 2011 drama starring Brad Pitt as Oakland A's general manager Billy Beane. The A's began preaching the value of on-base percentage way back in the 1980s, when general manager Sandy Alderson embraced the writings of Eric Walker, a former aerospace engineer who argued that offenses should be more concerned with avoiding outs than amassing base hits. The book and the movie just brought tremendous attention to the Athletics' philosophies.

At one point, the Oakland organization was so focused on plate discipline and running up pitch counts that the A's tinkered with incentives throughout the entire farm system. An Oakland prospect couldn't advance a rung in the minors or win an organizational award unless he walked in ten percent of his plate appearances or posted an OBP of .350 or better. Oakland development personnel eventually concluded that those markers were too rigid, and they dispensed with the standards. Nevertheless, the A's became renowned—and in some circles renounced—for teaching a take-take-take approach in the minors to try to develop high on-base hitters.

By the time the *Moneyball* movie was released, though, Oakland had changed its approach. Following the 2012 season, then-Oakland farm director Keith Lieppman told *Baseball America*: "We've almost gone 180 [degrees] from that mentality. The new plan is getting a pitch to hit. If that comes early in the count, then hit it. We were too narrow in our scope. We're much more aggressive than we were in the past."

Here's the moral of that story: Different strokes for different folks. If you talk to one manager, hitting coach, scout, statistician and so forth, patience at the plate may be preached as the way to make it to the next level or to thrive at the level you currently play. An equally good manager, hitting coach, scout, statistician and so forth, however, may preach a much more aggressive approach. The reality is that both are right and wrong. There is merit to both viewpoints, and both approaches work for many different hitters. The key is to know yourself and to learn when each approach should be utilized.

The key to a hitter's success is to be able to adjust to any type of approach that is presented. Be proactive, not reactive and realize that there is more than one way to skin a cat or to produce at the plate. If your team, organization or coach is adamant about a particular philosophy, accept it as a challenge and embrace the situation with a can-do attitude. Do not be hard-headed, un-coachable or defiant. If you do, you are only hurting yourself and your chances of being in the lineup.

A great, but difficult challenge is to take whatever philosophy, strategy or approach is given to you and to use it to your benefit and advantage. Remember that your attitude determines your altitude. In other words, your ability to maintain a good attitude will propel you higher and make the game far more enjoyable.

When you are asked to work counts and see more pitches, think about how that can benefit you and your team. For example:

- You may develop a better feel for the strike zone.
- In developing a more patient approach, you may also discover more of an ability to relax.
- You can practice your hitting position as you are taking pitches.
- You may become better two-strike hitters.
- You will have an opportunity to see all the types of pitches the opposing pitcher throws.

Conversely, if you are asked to be aggressive, the benefits may be:

- You have a better chance of hitting fastballs.
- Statistically, most damage is done in the first four pitches of an at-bat.
- You are in attack mode and are not likely to be caught looking at strike three.

Hitting in counts, ahead, even or behind. The two-strike approach

You are in a count every pitch of every at-bat. All hitters have success in different counts, and you typically have a better chance of being successful when you are ahead in the count or have less than two strikes. When a pitcher is behind in the count, he is more likely to throw a strike because he doesn't want to fall further behind or issue a walk. Obviously, you have a better chance to hit a strike than something out of the zone. Then we have the swing counts: 0-0, 1-1 and 2-2. The significance of these counts is that you are either going to be ahead in the count or behind as a result of the next pitch (excluding a foul ball on a 2-2 count). Finally, the "behind-the count" situations are 0-1, 0-2 and 1-2. When you are behind in the count you are in a tough spot because the pitcher doesn't have to throw a strike and he can expand his zone in an attempt to make you chase.

Here's the key to being competitive in counts: know the strike zone. That's easier said than done, but when you have a better feel for the strike zone, you have a better chance of swinging at good pitches and laying off pitches out of the zone. There are other variables involved such as the umpire and his strike zone, your timing, your mental state and your ego. But you want to start with an understanding of the strike zone that you control.

A wonderful approach is to work off of three balls, placing one directly in the middle of the plate and then placing a ball on each side of first ball. The reason you use three balls and not five is that the tendency is to expand the area where you are normally looking to hit a pitch by the distance of two baseballs. The time to maybe look at covering five balls is when you have two strikes and you must be aware of the whole plate. When you look for three balls, you will tend to swing at five. When you look for five balls then you will tend to swing at seven.

To understand the height of the strike zone, you can break it down into three areas: around the knees or low is one area; the thighs and waist is the second area; and around the belly button to below the uniform letters is the third. Most hitters have a particular area in which they feel more comfortable hitting. Seek pitches in specific areas according to whether you are ahead or behind in the count.

You can also consider the type of pitcher you are facing. Does he throws strikes or is he wild? Does he throw hard or is he crafty? Does he throw a curveball, a slider or changeup? Does he throw a sinker or a cutter? After you know the pitcher's arsenal and tendencies, you can look for specific pitches in certain areas. Some good rules to consider are:

- If a majority of his pitches move toward you or away from you, set your sights accordingly.
- Left-handed hitters facing a right-handed sinker/slider pitcher should work off the three balls and move them toward you one ball. That way, the sinker you look for will start inside and be over the plate. The sinker that starts away will run off the plate and be a ball.
- A right-handed hitter facing a right-handed sinker/slider pitcher should take three balls and move them away from you one ball. The sinker that starts away will have a better chance of being in the strike zone. The sinker that starts middle to in will run and be a ball.
- If the pitcher's main pitch moves away from you, bring three balls closer to you. If the pitcher's main pitch moves towards you, move the three balls away from you.
- If a pitcher has two quality pitches, one that may move away and one that may move in, leave the three balls in the middle.
- If a pitcher throws hard, four-seam fastballs, leave the balls in the middle.
- If a pitcher has a good straight change, look higher up in the zone.
- If a pitcher likes to pitch up in zone, then move your hitting target area down.

Obviously none of these are etched in stone, but a least it gives you some thoughts on how to attack different pitchers. With any of these approaches, the key is to commit to the area you are looking for and to work hard to not be teased or enticed into expanding your zone to help the pitcher. If you are ahead in the count, you can shrink your area a bit more as you move into hitter's counts. When you are behind the count, you may need to expand the zone a bit more, especially with two strikes. Just always make sure that you are totally committed and staying in the moment of "pitch to pitch" and avoid mechanical thoughts.

The strikeout epidemic

A big topic in baseball in more years is the strikeouts, which are happening at alarming rates. Strikeouts were once embarrassing for hitters; now they are acceptable. The reasons for the increased strikeouts in all levels of the game are better pitching, specialized, one-inning pitchers, more powerful pitchers, an increased focus on hitting home runs, over swinging with two strikes and so forth. In today's game, it is common to see hitters with 500 at-bats with 100 or more strikeouts during the course of a year. In essence, players are striking out once every four to five at bats or, on average, almost one time per game. This is an alarming and unacceptable rate in my book, so let's see if we can do something about it.

I challenge you not to simply accept the current strikeout rates and to be a better contact hitter. That doesn't mean you are never going to strike out, but I encourage you to be proactive and to limit your own strikeouts.

I worked with a hitter in the minor leagues who struck out 162 times during a full season in low-A ball. His overall numbers were decent, and he was a good run-producer. Our challenge to him was to cut down his strikeouts the following year by 20 percent. The key for him to do that was to shorten up with two strikes and to enter a more competitive mode. The following year, he cut his strikeouts to 125, which made him an even better run-producer. You are in control of your at-bats, and you control how you adjust your two-strike approach. Altering your approach can make you a better contact hitter, a better run-producer and can lead your teams to more wins. Here are some examples to consider in your two-strike approach:

- Choke up and shorten your swing.
- Spread your stance out.
- Take a no-stride approach.
- Utilize a secondary or "B" swing as opposed to an aggressive "A" swing.
- Commit to hitting the ball to the opposite field.
- Sit on the hardest pitch away.
- Live for another pitch.
- Simply make contact to work the count to your favor.

The whole idea with two strikes is to commit to one thought, one idea and one approach.

Many times when hitters struggle with two strikes it's because they have not committed 100 percent to any thought, and they are just in the box leaving things up to chance. If you are struggling, commit to one thought other than what you've been doing. Also make sure that your inner voice is feeding you positive and truthful thoughts.

If you tell yourself you are not good at hitting with two strikes, you are dooming yourself to failure. A proactive approach would be to tell yourself that the next time you are in a two-strike situation, you are going to commit to this or that. Take a positive outlook do something different than what you have been doing if that has not worked. If you are a good two-strike hitter and have a solid plan, see if you can get better. Remember in everything you do, you can improve. Being a good two-strike hitter is mental. It's a belief, it's a way you choose to think, and it's a choice that you control.

Your in-game plan or approach

Your plan in the batter's box supersedes any and every aspect of the hitting task. It's all about the mind, and what you think about is the most important element of your game. Throughout the history of the game, players with all types of swings and mechanisms have been successful, regardless of whether they look good or not. But the common denominator that has allowed all hitters to be successful is belief—a belief in their swing, a belief their ability, a belief that they will be successful in this moment.

A good question to ask yourself is this: "What is your definition of success at the plate?" Is it just getting hits and driving in runs? Is it just about the end result? If so, you may need to take a step back and define success in a different way. Define success in a way that you are in control. The one most powerful thing that God has blessed you with is your mind. You have the ability to control your mind if you choose do so. Instead of defining success at the plate merely by the end result of an at-bat, try defining success one swing at a time. Did you commit to thinking about just one thing? Did you execute one thought for one pitch? If so, then that is an example of a successful approach to that pitch, whether you took the pitch or lined it into the gap for an RBI double.

As you are hitting, you want to work to reach attainable goals. It is much more likely to be able to execute a thought for one pitch than hit a pitch 400 feet. Control what you can control and let the uncontrollable take care of itself. You can't control if a ball you hit lands for a hit, but you can control the thought you have before the pitch and you can control making good solid contact. Simply commit to one solid thought, and allow that thought to be your plan at the plate. This thought is different for each and every one of us and has to match your style and your abilities. The thought could be practically anything, such as:

- Relax
- Be smooth
- Hit down through the ball
- Hit a strike
- Work through the middle of field
- Work to hit ball to right center
- Be on time
- Start off the pitcher
- Look middle in
- Look middle away
- Hit a fastball
- Relax the front shoulder
- Breathe

One ten-year-old I worked with was struggling and kept swinging and missing pitches. His confidence was down and he had no chance of success. We came to the conclusion that his mind needed to be redirected from "I can't make contact" to "it's a given that I can make contact." I encouraged him to think about a 1-2 approach. One represented separating and two was the actual swing. Instead of being fearful of not making contact, he began tearing the cover off the ball. He replaced the negative thought with a thought he could execute.

Another example involves an MLB player who was struggling and kept thinking it was his mechanics. The more he grinded on mechanics, the tighter and tenser he became. When he was truthful about his in-game thoughts, he acknowledged thinking this: "I am rolling over and grounding to short and third twice a game, which feels like crap." But the reality is that it was not his swing or the mechanics that was the problem. It was his thought process. The suggestion was made to totally commit to hitting the ball to right center. His angry, sarcastic reply was, "Fine, I will just commit to right center!" He went 3-for-4 that game with a homer. He let go of the mechanical doubt and trusted the thought. Sometimes, it's not that simple. Other times it is. We just have to accept it and commit one pitch at a time.

Another example is of a high school hitter who was pulling off pitches and trying to do too much because he was told he needed to start hitting for power. It's a tough task to ask a hitter to all of a sudden start hitting for power. So the commitment was made to look middle away and expect to get a pitch to hit there. He was 90 percent committed, but not 100 percent committed. He later acknowledged, "I was committed to middle away, but in the back of my mind I thought about the pitch on the inner half that I knew I could drive over the plate. So the problem continued with pulling off the ball." You must "sell out" to one thought for it to work.

Finally, after a couple of games, this high schooler finally said "Ok, I am going to commit to middle away and let the inner half pitch go." He then was able to stay square long enough and begin swinging better.

Quality/productive at bats

Beauty is in the eye of the beholder. So are quality at-bats. A coach, instructor or parent may view a quality at-bat differently than you assess your own at-bat. For most people, a quality at-bat is when you get a hit, hit a ball hard, draw a walk, are hit by a pitch, execute in a successful situation or see seven or more pitches. But another way you can look at these kinds of at bats is by gauging your thought process or game plan. So it is possible for you to have a quality at-bat in your own view, as opposed to the typical way it might be measured. This is a big way in which you can stay positive, regardless of the end results. You want to be able to find positives out of every at-bat, and when you can assess your thought process and how committed you were, you can work to change your thinking or continue to maintain it.

In evaluating your at-bats, always remember that a hit is a hit, no matter how it comes. Whether it's a line drive in the gaps, a bloop single or a 25-hopper that squeaks through the middle, a hit is a hit and you will take every one of them. A hard-hit ball that is squared up is actually what you strive to do every at-bat.

Drawing a walk gets you on base. It tells you that you didn't swing at pitches out of the zone. Even when you are intentionally walked, it's a quality at-bat. The opposing team chose not to pitch to you. Getting hit by a pitch speaks for itself. It's the price you paid to get on base. Successfully executing in a situation is the most productive at-bat you will have because it is a team at-bat and those kinds of at-bats are essential to scoring runs. Those are situations such as moving a runner from second base to third with no outs. You are sacrificing your at-bat by moving the runner into better scoring position. Another situation is with the runner at third base with less than two outs. You want to score the runner any way you can. If the infield is playing back or the infield is playing in, you want to put the ball in play in a way that gets the runner to cross home plate. Another huge situation is having runners in scoring position with two outs. This is the hardest RBI to get in baseball because there are two outs, but it is probably the most crippling to the other team. When you have at-bats that extend to seven or more pitches, view those as quality at-bats because you have made the pitcher work extra.

In higher levels of baseball, there is a big emphasis on quality at-bats because obviously as you play at higher levels, the game is more difficult and the need for productive at-bats becomes more valuable.

The giveaway at bats

The power of regret is something we deal with in our daily life, as well as in baseball. As hitters, how many times do you go back to the dugout after an at-bat and realize how you just messed up? You swung at a bad pitch or froze on a pitch right down the middle. Then you go home after the game thinking about how bad your at-bats were because you did this or didn't do that. The regrets come in droves.

These at bats are called giveaways. Most players give at-bats away more than they realize. It was once stated by arguably the best MLB hitting coach that MLB hitters give away one at-bat every game. Then he said that in the minor leagues, hitters give away two at-bats every game. Think about that. If a MLB hitter gives away one at-bat a game, that amounts to seven per week, 30 a month and 180 over the course of a season. A minor league hitter giving away two at-bats a night amounts to 14 a week, 60 a month and 360 at season. That's absolutely mind boggling. Obviously, the less at-bats you give away, the better hitter you will be. Here are some of the ways players typically give away at-bats:

- Lack of commitment to a game plan
- Not present in the at bat
- Late with timing
- Swinging at a bad pitch
- Trying to do too much
- Trying to hit a ball too hard
- Worried about not getting hits
- Worried about playing the next game
- Worried about getting cut
- Fear of what our parents will say
- Fear of what our coach thinks about us
- Flaw in swing
- Anxious or nervous
- Fear of failure
- Fear of success
- Our team is way behind in the score
- Our team is way ahead in the score
- Let's just get this game over with
- Too many thoughts in your head

All or some of these reasons happen to each of us from time to time. The first step to avoiding these pitfalls is being accountable and being totally honest about the reasons you give away at-bats. Too many hitters do not want to admit the reason because they may look or give the impression that they are weak or vulnerable. The reality is that you need to admit your flaws so you can make the adjustment and figure out how to minimize or eliminate your issues. Another key is to train yourself to value every at-bat, regardless of whether you have three hits in a game or are in an 0-for-10 slump. And don't let emotions interfere with at-bats, regardless of whether or not you are bored with a game, fearful of an opposing pitcher, anxious to move on to the next inning or anything else of the sort. Value every at-bat in every game.

Emotions like arrogance, cockiness, fear, anxiety, frustration, anger, jealousy and envy cloud your mind and deter you from controlling your thoughts and ideas. They take your focus away from the moment and lead you to giving away at-bats. To be in the moment of your at-bats, emotions must be put on the back burner. The ability to do that comes from the strength of your mind that will allow you to commit to the plan. The thing you want to understand is the length of time you want to commit to your plan only lasts about five seconds. That's how long a pitch lasts. That's why it's important to go one pitch at a time. Surely, you can commit to a plan for five seconds at a time, right? If you can do that and value every at-bat, you can become a much better hitter right away!

PART 2

During my 18 years I came to bat almost 10,000 times. I struck out about 1,700 times and walked maybe 1,800 times. You figure a ballplayer will average about 500 at bats a season. That means I played seven years without ever hitting the ball.
— *Mickey Mantle, 1970*

Bad habits are easier to abandon today than tomorrow.
— *Yiddish Proverb*

You have to expect things of yourself before you can do them.

— *Michael Jordan*

Chapter 7
Mechanical disciplines

Like diets, workout plans, medical advice and political opinions on social media, there are literally hundreds upon hundreds of different philosophies that are available to hitters if they choose to do a little research online. Likewise, there are books, videos and clinics led by numerous different coaches implementing various different programs. The problem is that, because we all have access to such an abundance of information, hitters tend to walk to the plate and step into the batter's box with information overload. I can practically see the wheels spinning inside the heads of so many hitters as they attempt to be successful at the plate.

Watching these confused youngsters, as they attempt to process so much information, as the ball leaves the pitcher's hand reminds me of the old 1980s public service announcements that were produced by the Partnership for a Drug-Free America in which a close up was shown of an egg was into a hot frying pan. The accompanying voiceover stated: "OK, last time. This is drugs. This is your brain on drugs. Any questions?"

At any level, too much information to process at the plate inevitably leads a hitter to scrambled and/or fried minds. Keep it simple. Keep it concise. And it's probably wise to keep yourself off the Internet in search of hitting solutions.

As we discuss the one-two steps, keep your swing in the back of your mind and see how these thoughts and ideas apply to you. Some thoughts will be familiar to you, while others will be new to you and some may not apply. This approach is designed to adjust and adapt to each individual... as opposed to the individual hitter adapting to the approach.

The one-two step sequence is applicable to every style of hitter. Whether you utilize a leg kick, a toe tap, hitting with rhythm or a conventional mode (getting foot down early), any style becomes much easier if you simply break down the sequence of your swing. It becomes easier to improve when there are simple steps to the swing. As you go through these steps, it is good to keep in mind the points made in the mental disciplines chapters because your mental state and thought process has a direct connection to your mechanics.

Step 1: Timing of the Separation

The first step of the swing process is the timing of the separation. We can talk about timing in a variety of ways and terms to allow it to apply to any style. The terms "being on time" or "being late" are often used loosely, and you may not always be able to pinpoint exactly why your timing is on or off. But there are essentially three ways that timing is affected:

- How you start your sequence off the pitcher's windup (getting started off the pitcher)
- Making an extra movement in your preparation to hit or featuring an extra body move
- Simply having way too many thoughts that are flying around in your head.

Timing is often dictated by the pitcher's break of the hands in their delivery. Another way to start your timing is when the pitcher's front leg begins moving down toward the plate. There are other terms that can be used to help define being "on time." You can work to be in rhythm with the pitcher or just move or dance with them. Like a dance partner, when the pitcher starts, you start. When they break their hands, you break your hands.

One thing you must understand is that timing is always constant. It starts off the pitcher's motion, as a cue or a trigger. When you have no cue on the start of your separation, you tend to become rigid and robotic. Either that, or you have too much movement in your body, resulting in a loss of balance and/or control. Keep your cue the same, regardless whether a pitcher is throwing hard or slow. Your adjustment can be based on how the speed of the pitch is absorbed. Fast pitchers will make the duration of your separation shorter, while slow pitchers will cause your duration to be a bit longer.

While it's true that you can never start too early, there needs to be some smoothness or balance to how you start. If you start early and create more time, then be cautious not to place too much weight on your back leg because this causes you to create a spring-like effect with your back leg. When you place too much weight back, you tend to compress the spring and try to create balance. The end result is the spring shooting our weight forward, which results in over-striding or opening up your front side. Other times, the spring collapses and makes you fall back on your heels and open up.

Your rhythm dictates your timing, and it is good to remember that rhythm is uniquely individual. It is your own personal rhythm that functions for you and is not forced. Some hitters have rhythm in the hands or the bat, while others have more rhythm in their legs. Still, some hitters will match up the rhythm in hands with the rhythm in the legs. There is no definitive right or wrong way. It's all about your own style. Stay relaxed and committed to a thought or plan, because that tends to make you confident, and when you are confident is when your rhythm is natural and works on its own. Conversely, when you are in a state of anxiety or panic, your rhythm tends to speed up, becomes awkward or disappears altogether. That is when it becomes obvious to practically anyone in the ballpark that you are not feeling your best. It's your body language that dictates how you feel, so even if you are not feeling it, "fake it until you make it." You can give the impression that you feel great when in reality you don't. Another way to regain rhythm is to take a deep breath and let it out slowly. This will allow everything to slow down and your body tends to return to the normal state you seek. Rhythm is timing, and it is one of the few things you completely control. When you lean toward being more relaxed and smooth, you will develop more natural rhythm.

As you work your timing through your rhythm, it is important to understand how you separate through rhythm. Separation is also referred to as "the load." When you start the process of separating or loading, understand that this is what leads you into a strong hitting position. Your hands work back toward the catcher as your stride works in the direction of the pitcher. Imagine having a rubber band tied from the knob of the bat to your front toe. When you separate or load, you stretch the rubber band.

Another phrase about rhythm states, "Walking away from your hands." This is where I tend to see the biggest issues or problems with young hitters because the tendency is to separate or load by pushing too much weight to the back leg, which is overloading. There is more detail about weight distribution in the next chapter, but briefly in regards to the one-two step sequence. A good question to ask yourself is: "When I start the process of separating, do I feel more weight on my back leg or is there tension or tightness in my back knee?" There should be a 60-40 weight distribution. It can benefit a hitter more if the thought is more in terms of a 50-50 or 55-45 distribution. Hitters are well known for over exaggerating things, however, so if you are working to get to 60-40, you may in reality be getting to more of 70-30 or 80-20. When your weight shifts too much to your back leg, it negatively impacts quite a few things, but especially the bat path and how short you can stay to the ball. When you overload, you tend to slide your body to the front side (toward the pitcher). This makes you open your front side sooner and makes your hands drag behind.

One of the simplest things to do is to concentrate on the balance of the weight of your legs from side to side. A couple of areas that can be the focus are either feeling the weight on the balls of your feet or on the inside part of your thighs.

The other thing that can happen is that your weight shifts too far on the outside of your back foot, which makes you open early. Consequently, the bat path tends to work up and under pitches. A good rule of thumb is when your separation is complete and your front foot hits the ground, your back side and hands are the things that

move first toward the pitch. When you have proper weight distribution, your hands and back side work more in sync and your swing comes out shorter, quicker and more powerful. You are, in essence, creating space between you and the ball, which gives you more time to react to the pitch. You also are allowing your weight to stay centered, keeping your head steady, which allows you to work more balanced. Watch a figure skater do a one-legged spin at the conclusion of a routine. As the skater begins the rotation, both arms are outstretched and one leg is pointed out. As the arms and leg get closer to the body, the spin increases in velocity. It becomes a rapid movement. This is similar to when the hitter keeps his weight more in the center of the body. The turn from the back side and hands is tighter and creates a quicker, more powerful move through the pitch. It's a more compact swing.

As you relate this to your swing, think about your mechanism or style of your separation. If your style includes a leg kick or tap, the separation happens in a little different fashion than hitting with rhythm or the conventional mode. The front leg is moving back first as the initial move, which is called a "controlled negative move." Then, as the front leg or foot begins working toward the pitcher, the hands begin to work the stretch of the rubber band. If the hands start back as the front leg is working back, the hands may tend to go too far back. Consequently, when the front foot starts forward, there is not much of a counterbalance. The body tends to move forward too much.

There are exceptions to every rule, so hitters will have variations to this. But it is important to remember that the hands separating back are an important move to give you balance and the ability to stay behind the ball. Many times, as a hitter initiates the leg kick or tap, the hands may make a move down or even bounce. Then, as the stride goes forward, this allows the separation to occur together. For example, Josh Donaldson leg kicks. When he starts his leg kick, his hands move down toward his belly button. Then as he starts the stride, his hands begin working back and a solid stretch of the band occurs—a balance and counter balance.

Alfonso Soriano didn't do much with his hands, but as he leg kicked and the stride foot started forward, his counterbalance was a slight cock of the bat, pointing his bat head a bit toward the pitcher. This gave him balance to swing. Prince Fielder started his swing with a tap back. As he tapped, his hands didn't do much. But to generate a little rhythm, Fielder moved his hands back just a bit as his stride foot went forward, almost like his body was moving forward to stride and he moved away from his hands to create great balance before the swing.

The other mechanism or style of hitting is with rhythm/conventional. As the separation occurs, it is more at the same time and hitters tend to go into the stretch sooner. There is not as much delay when the hands work back, creating a balance or counter balance. It is usually much easier to repeat the conventional approach because you are basically working directly into separation. This way there is a pause as you separate, which allows you to have your feet on the ground and generates a better opportunity to keep your body square and in a strong hitting position. Focus on not feeling rushed or hurried with your timing which will lead you toward feeling tense, and the result is a tension-filled, slower swing.

Again, there is more detail about the grip in Chapter 8, but one point that is often overlooked in properly separating is the grip or how you hold the bat. An improper grip impacts how far you separate back, as well as the direction you take the hands back. An improper grip can make you go too far back and create an arm bar or cause you to go too far behind your body and create a closing off or flying open movement. Check your grip by making sure you have the handle in between your palm and fingers. If you are "choking" the bat, you will have less feel and looseness. As such, the swing isn't as compact and in control as you want it. You can align your grip by pointing your pointer fingers straight up to the sky. This allows our wrists to be in a cocked, anchored angle and it allows you to create more whip and speed. As you separate, your fingers should still be working in the direction of the sky. This also allows the front elbow to stay in a more relaxed position and keeps it out of the way. Monitor that both wrists do not end up flat and even with the forearms. There should be about a right angle at the wrist.

STEP 2 STRONG HITTING POSITION

The second step in the hitting sequence is to move into a strong hitting position. This means you should be in a balanced, athletic position. Simulate jumping as high as you possibly can, guarding someone in basketball or tackling someone in football. Your knees are flexed and your weight is on the inside of the balls of your feet, inside your thighs. Again, think of a figure skater as she does a turn to end the routine. As she begins the turn her arms and one leg are outstretched away from the center of her body. As she brings the arms and leg closer to center, the turn becomes faster and faster. This is the same thing that happens with your swing. When you are close to center with your weight, your hands and lower half work together. The result is a faster, more powerful and compact swing. Think about how powerful that is to your state of mind and the peace you gain knowing you are short and compact with your swing.

Many hitters tend to torque and twist in their stance so much that when they are finished separating, they are not in a strong athletic position. Hitting a baseball is one of the most difficult things to do in any sport. It only makes it

Mechanical disciplines

harder if you do not place your body in position to anticipate anything and be ready to attack.

When I talk about being in a strong athletic position, I refer to this as "being square," which is the most optimum position for consistently hitting a pitch. That means that after you have separated, your body is balanced and level. If you can, take your bat in this position after separating and check your alignment by lining your bat at your feet. You can see the direction of where your stride has gone by where the bat is pointing. Then place your bat at your knees and check alignment and direction, analyzing your hips and your shoulders. If you can visualize standing in a box or a door jam, you should feel the balance and alignment of your body "being squared up." When you are square, it will allow you to let the ball travel more because your swing will come out shorter and quicker.

When your front side is open or opens early, your contact point tends to either be too far out in front or too far back in the zone. This is referred to as being in between: late on fastballs and early on off-speed pitches. Your contact point should be around your front foot, and when your front foot is square, your contact point is more consistent. When your front foot opens, you tend to want to swing earlier. Another way to look at it is if your front side opens, then your swing will work out and around the pitch. As you stride to be square, you should work to land on the instep of the front foot or the inside of your front big toe. The term "stick it" or land with your instep is applicable. Envision your front foot working like a door stopper. The rubber triangle wedges under the door and makes it stay in place. Relating it to our body, the front foot keeps you from going forward or drifting if you stick it. That allows your hands and back side to take you to the ball and stay centered.

As the stride foot lands on the instep, the front foot should be close to parallel with the front of the plate, although some hitters land at more of a 45-degree angle. The idea is to ensure that the front hip and shoulder stay square until the hands and back leg clear them out of the way. When the actual swing begins, you want to understand how your "connection" keeps you short, compact and direct to the ball. The reality is most hitters want to attack and drive balls thinking about their hands. But they tend to get forward with their weight a bit early, and it lends to making contact too far out in front. The result is hitting over the top or underneath the ball.

When you understand that the hands and back leg work together, then the body stays more centered and a space is created between the chest and the ball. This allows you to work more inside and through the ball, and it also allows the contact point to be closer to your front foot. That is where you create the fastest part of your swing. The terms "whip," "flick" or "swish" of the bat is where you want your consistent contact point.

The bat path

Remember that you will never go wrong working to shorten your path through the hitting area, as a compact swing is typically the best swing. While it is true that a good, fundamental swing has some length through the hitting area or stays through the hitting area, many times that is a direct result of what has happened beforehand.

As you separate and move to your hitting position, the next step in the sequence is to recognize what type of pitch you are seeing and its location. This is where the decision-

Mechanical disciplines

making process occurs. You have more time, and it gives you more confidence to be relaxed and natural. Once the separation process is complete, think about how you will work into the hitting area. Your first move should be in a downward angle toward the pitch. I am not talking about chopping down. The downhill move only happens for the first 12 inches or so of the swing. After that, the barrel is following your hand path, and in turn, begins to lag into the hitting area. Too early of a lag will result in foul balls or swings and misses.

Too many times I hear people say that when you foul a ball straight back, it's a good swing and you just missed. It is not a good swing because it is a pitch you should have driven somewhere between the lines. When you foul balls straight back or miss them, it will give the feeling that you are swinging up or under the ball. This is usually the case when hitters are in a bit of a downslide. A simple thought can get you back to being more direct to the ball. Pick your simple thought. Any one of these will work:

- Hit down through the ball
- Hit the top of the ball
- Hit a hard ground ball
- Hit low line drives
- Hit the ball with back spin

A good example of this is of a big leaguer who had come off of a serious injury. He was taking batting practice preparing for game and couldn't barrel-up the ball. He was hitting plenty of pop ups in the cage and weak fly balls. It was suggested to him to try and hit on top of ball. He said, "My swing doesn't work that way. My swing is flat, which allows me to drive balls into the gaps." So the suggestion was altered, challenging him to see how many line drives he could hit through the outfield wall. Not to the wall, but through it. His reply: "Yeah I can do that." The next two rounds resulted in line drive all over the field and a couple in the seats.

It's all about the perception and perspective of the individual hitter. One of the aforementioned thoughts can be the difference in feeling the good swing or not. The thought can be carried over into the game as your one thought.

As you work to be shorter to the ball, allow your contact point to be closer to your front foot, which allows you to hit through the ball. When you work shorter to the ball, the finish of the swing will be a bit higher. Some hitters finish close to level with the shoulders and some finish higher than the shoulders.

Another way to check and see if your swing is shorter is to check your balance at completion. If you are falling back or away from the plate, then your swing is working up or around. If you are falling too far toward the plate while losing your balance then you may be working out and around the ball. The ideal finish is with your chest squared to the pitcher's mound and a solid foundation giving you great balance.

As you focus on your bat path, it is important to remember the things that affect it. Your front hip direction is your biggest indicator. When your front hip is pointed in the direction of the pitcher or the middle of the field, there is a good chance your swing will work toward the middle of the field. If your hips are pointed upward or too much toward the plate or away from plate, then your bat path will be affected by your hand path starting out or up. Another way your bat path is affected is when you try to put too much effort or power in the swing. Still, another reason is when you try to hit too much to the opposite field or too much to the pull side of the field.

When you work the middle of the field, it opens up both sides and gives you more room to find base hits. Use all of the field by starting with the biggest part: centerfield.

The Lower Half

When I talk about the lower half, please understand that balance is the most crucial part of utilizing it consistently. The lower half needs to be repeated often in all the pregame work and batting practice to allow the feeling to be more consistent. With proper practice and repetition of lower half, it can become second nature. You will gain confidence that reveals itself in games…the way you want it.

One of the most powerful things you can do with your lower half is to pinch your knees to ensure a flexed athletic position. Whatever your style, understand that you use the lower half to move into an athletic hitting position so you can use the back leg or back side to take you to the ball.

As you separate into your stride—and once the front foot lands on the ground—the back leg will initiate the start of the swing. It is important to note that when your front foot hits the ground, you want to maintain a square or closed position with your front side. The more square you land, the shorter and more powerful your swing will be. If you land a bit open, then your backside will work toward the plate and will cause your swing to be longer.

When you start the move into the pitch, your goal should be to work the back hip, back knee and back foot together toward the hitting area. Your back hip should work fairly even and level to keep your hands above the ball. When the back hip starts working under the front hip, you tend to create a longer swing and a cave-in with the back knee.

Every hitter is different in how they are able to make this move. Some hitters will think about taking the back hip to the ball, while others will think about pivoting the back foot. If you can think about your hip or your back foot working exactly together with your hands, then you have a cleaner more fluid swing and you have a better chance of:

- Staying behind the ball
- Working shorter and more direct to ball
- Staying balanced
- Driving the ball
- Hitting line drives with backspin

Not every swing will be exactly the same, but when you work to repeat this, it will allow for a more consistent swing. It is good to note that your finish will dictate how consistent you are. When you make contact and fall back, we call this a recoil, which gives you a false sense of balance. When you complete the swing, you should be able to hold your finish at that point with complete balance and no extra movements. Again, this is the ideal way you want to practice.

This doesn't mean that you should think about this in an actual game. That is where the trust in your practice takes over.

"It is not the beauty of a building you should look at; it's the construction of the foundation that will stand the test of time."

– David Allan Coe

"When the roots are deep, there is no reason to fear the wind."

– Chinese proverb

Chapter 8
More Mechanical disciplines

On April 10, 1912, RMS Titanic began its maiden voyage, leaving Southampton on the southern coast of England for New York City. Titanic carried 2,224 passengers and 885 crew members, including some of the wealthiest people in the world, as well as hundreds of emigrants from Great Britain, Ireland and elsewhere throughout Europe seeking a new life in North America. The largest and most high-profile passenger liner in service at that time, Titanic was revered by the masses around the globe and was said to be "unsinkable." Perhaps that's why, despite receiving six warnings of sea ice on the night of April 14, Captain Edward John Smith, kept travelling near Titanic's maximum speed when her lookouts sighted an iceberg.

The problem with an iceberg, of course, is that typically only one-tenth of the volume is above water. The other 90 percent of the iceberg is below the water. Once the crew members of Titanic spotted the portion of the iceberg above the water, it was too late.

Unable to turn quickly enough, Titanic suffered a glancing blow that buckled her starboard (right) side and opened five of her 16 compartments to the sea. Titanic had been designed to stay afloat with four of her forward compartments flooded, but no more. Four days and about 375 miles into her maiden voyage, Titanic hit an iceberg at 11:40 p.m. ship's time. At 2:20 a.m., she broke apart and floundered. Approximately 1,500 people died that morning when the unsinkable ship sank.

Here's the point: No matter how big you are, how much publicity you receive or how invincible you may believe yourself to be, you may be doomed and headed for destruction if you are not constantly aware of foundational issues.

More Mechanical disciplines

Your stance is a key factor in developing and maintaining consistently in your swing. Each hitter has their own unique style that fits to the way their swing functions. When we watch MLB hitters, you see all different variations from Brandon Phillips setting up with a wide base and bent over a bit, to Chris Davis who stands with a narrow base and is more upright. Regardless of the stance, make sure to align your setup with the way the mechanics of your swing works. If you are a leg-kick hitter, who lifts the front foot up or back then strides to hit, or tap hitter, who takes a step back toward the back foot and then strides, be careful to avoid being too wide with your feet or too close in alignment. If you are a rhythm hitter or early strider, be careful to avoid being too narrow with your feet.

Although there is no definitive way to set up for each individual, it needs to be consistent and relatively the same every time you hit. It's your own unique, individual stance, and you should be aware of how wide your feet are set up. You should be aware if your feet are in a straight line toward the pitcher, slightly open or slightly closed. Notice how much weight is on your front or back leg. Be aware of the direction your shoulders are pointing. Pay close attention to where your hand position is in relation to your head/back shoulder. Finally, take note of your head position. Do you have both eyes looking at the pitcher or are you closing off the back eye? Is your head upright, tilted back or tilted forward?

Memorize your stance and how it feels because over the course of a week or a month, there tends to be subtle movements that may make you shift your stance slightly or drastically. Check your stance in front of a mirror so you can have a visual for your stance. Video is also a good way of keeping tabs on your stance. You will benefit from seeing your stance from the dugout view, as well as from the pitcher's view. Those perspectives can provide the answer to difficulties if your swing isn't feeling good.

Start with your feet. A good way to gauge proper feet positioning is to get in your stance where you feel athletic and comfortable. Then take your bat and place it on the ground in front of your toes pointing from the catcher to the pitcher. Place the knob of the bat in front of your back foot. Then measure how wide your feet are apart from each other. Find a letter or emblem on the barrel of your bat and use that like a ruler to know how wide your feet should be. For most hitters—and there are exceptions—the feet should not be wider than the length of the bat. If your feet are wider than the length of the bat, your legs tend to get stiff and tense, and your stride will take you even wider. As a result, it will be more difficult to use your backside turn, weight shift or pivot into ball. Whether you use an open stance or close stance, using your bat to measure is still in order.

Also be aware of the direction your toes are pointing. For most hitters, you want to have your toes pointing straight ahead in the direction of the plate. This helps keep your hips and shoulders in line with the pitcher and gives you better balance. If your feet are pointing out like a waddling duck, then your weight tends to move to your heels, and it will be difficult to maintain a balanced swing. If your toes are pointing inward (pigeon toed), then your weight tends to move toward your toes, which is better than a duck-footed setup. It is better to have your balance move toward the plate and the hitting area as opposed to back and away from it. No matter if your stance is open or closed, your feet should still be straight to inward. The tendency for hitters in an open stance is that the front foot opens and points toward the first baseman for right-handed hitters and toward third for left-handed hitters. This type of set-up will make you leak forward. For the closed-stance hitter, your front foot typically points back in the direction of the catcher and also tends to make you start with your front hip and shoulder too closed. That causes you to open up sooner and then makes you fall back away from the hitting area.

On to the knees

Shifting the focus from your feet, remember that one of the most powerful things you can do for your stance is to pinch your knees toward each other or work to keep them inside your feet. Without thinking, that keeps your body centered and allows you to have much more balance. As you pinch your knees, remember that your knee caps should stay straight ahead, not pointing inward or outward. When your knee caps point out, your weight moves to the outside of your feet and makes it difficult to keep your balance. If the knee caps are pointed inward too much it causes you to turn with your hips and shoulders.

For a hitter who is flexible, pinching the knees will be fairly easy. But guard against turning the knee caps too far in or your pivot will not work as easily. For the hitter who isn't as flexible, then pinching the knees can be a bit of a strain and will cause discomfort. In addition to stretching more, less-flexible hitters should turn their toes in more (pigeon toed), which will help keep your weight inside of your feet.

Hips

Moving further up the body, it's important to understand that your hip line or hip direction will dictate the direction of which way your swing will go. When you separate and land on the ground with your stride foot, the ideal position is to have the hips level and in direct line with the pitcher. The problem arises when your stride foot hits the ground and your hips are pointed outward, inward or upward. All three of those positions will cause the bat to take longer to get to the hitting area and usually the bat path is upward. Some of the causes to these three positions can be attributed to being late with your timing, having too much weight on your front side or back side, striding too much in, striding too much out or taking too big of a stride.

Shoulders and Hands

Many of the issues in hitting can be directly related to the shoulders, which work directly with your hands. Typically, the biggest issue with the front shoulder is it usually is the first thing that moves when you don't have a good swing. The back shoulder then tends to dip down and work under the direction of the pitch. Many shoulder issues are a result of what your hands are doing in your setup, separation and swing. When examining your set-up, check where your hands are in relation to your head and back shoulder. Many times your hands are set up too far back, which results in front shoulder tightness and tension.

Sometimes when you carry your hands too high, you can create the same type of front shoulder tightness. When your hands are too low, it may relieve the tension, but your front shoulder starts angling upward. Also if your hands start too far away from your body and toward the plate, then your shoulders sag, which affects how your posture is aligned.

A good starting place with your hands is fairly close to your back cheek or back ear. This keeps the bat knob pointing in the direction of the plate and perpendicular to your shoulders. This will eliminate shoulder tension and will give you a better opportunity to separate back in the direction of the pitcher.

Another consideration is to start your hands around chin level or below the ear. This will give you a better opportunity to separate back or maybe even a little bit up. When your hands start higher, your tendency is to separate downward, which makes the front shoulder tilt upward and the back shoulder tilt downward. There are exceptions to every rule, but usually those exceptions are rare and unorthodox.

Posture

Posture is extremely important in being able to repeat your swing. It all goes back to being an athlete and being in an athletic position as consistently as possible. Being in an athletic position is simply putting your body in the best position possible to be ready to react and move in the best possible way. Your legs should be flexed and agile, strong and stable. Your weight should be on the balls of your feet, not the heels or toes. Your weight should be balanced toward the insides of your feet or even your inner thighs to ensure you are centered.

Your upper body can be mostly related to your spine. You want a straight spine and for your rear end to be sticking out to some extent. You should feel the lower back a bit arched, which allows your chest to stick out a bit more while rolling your shoulders back.

Weight distribution

I am often asked these questions by hitters: Should I start with more weight on the back leg? Should I start more in the middle? Or should I start with more weight on our front leg?

These are tough questions to answer because everyone is different, but the way your weight is distributed in your lower half will definitely affect your swing. It can make it shorter or longer. Weight distribution can make the swing uphill or downhill. It will also affect whether you stay longer through the hitting area or are working in and out of it.

Whenever hitters feel like their bodies are going forward, they want to stop it by putting more weight on their back leg or "staying back." I've seen many hitters attempt to put all their weight on their back leg to keep them from going forward. But when you put more weight on your back leg, you create pressure and tension in the back knee. That forces your back knee to become like a spring. When you compress a spring, it becomes more difficult to control and one of two things will happen:

1. When you get ready to hit, the tension in your knee or the spring will open up and make you go forward even more. It will release and you end up straightening your back leg toward the pitcher. This will cause you to open up faster, and it makes your swing work longer and slower.

2. The other thing that can happen with all your weight on your back leg and tension in the knee is that it causes you to fall back and place more weight on your heels. As such, you open up and swing up and around the ball. This is called overloading the back side.

Make sure you understand the cause and effect of this action. What goes back tends to go forward, what goes down tends to go up, and sometimes what goes back stays back… and balance is lost.

As you think about your own swing and how this relates to it, remember some important points. If you can pinch your knees in an athletic position, you have a better chance of staying balanced and not being overloaded. Feel the weight of your body on the insides of the balls of your feet. That allows you to stay centered with your weight. Another point to remember is when you separate and feel your weight "load up," make sure to keep the tension out of your back knee. Feel it more on the inside of the back of your foot or more on the inner, upper thigh of your back leg. This will keep the back leg strong and stable and it will eliminate extra movement going forward. This also helps keep your front side in because you won't have a slide forward in your body. And when you have issues with your front side (flying open or going forward), you can fix the issue by controlling the back leg or back side and controlling where your weight is. In the same sense, you can fix the back side by keeping the front side square and more relaxed, which will help with the back side.

The grip

How you hold the bat makes a huge difference on many fronts. Your hand position in your stance determines how you separate and how the bat enters and works through the hitting area. Many hitters will think about where the elbows are in regard to hand position setup, but it is important to understand that the grip and the wrist angles are what control or affect how the elbows become involved with the swing.

When you grab the bat, make sure to set the handle of the bat primarily in the top part of your palm where the finger joints begin. Although many suggest to hold the bat in finger tips, sometimes that makes your grip weaker. On the flip side, when you place the handle of the bat primarily in your palms, you tend to choke the bat handle, which results in a stiffer, restricted swing.

A good way to check where the handle of the bat sits in your hands is to set up in the batter's box and hold the bat in your hand like you were going to hit a golf ball, with the end of the bat touching the ground. Open your hands so you can see the palms of your hands. Line up the handle of your bat with the joints where your fingers start and then grab the bat. Bring the barrel straight at your nose and proceed to lay the bat on your back shoulder.

Another nice checkpoint is to hold the bat on your shoulder and proceed to take both pointer fingers off the handle and point them towards the sky. If your fingers are crisscrossed and pointing opposite directions then your grip isn't as strong as it can be. The old adage of lining up your "door-knocking knuckles" is also a great way to check your grip. Even a little overlap in lining knuckles up is good, but it is preferred that the top hand be more overlapped toward the pitcher.

As you develop a stronger grip, you will be able to take your hands back (or separate) in a better direction to position your hands in a stronger launch position. Obviously, if your grip is weakened with either hand, it may result in extra movement in your separation, whether it's up, down, too far away from your body or too far behind your body. When the bottom hand is properly gripped, the back of the hand is facing more toward the pitcher and the front elbow is closer to your ribs, giving you a better chance of falling in place and not leading the knob into the hitting area. The same with the top hand when it is properly gripped, the back of the hand is facing toward the backstop. The problem begins when the backs of both hands will tend to point upward towards the sky and definitely affects our swing and the direction it goes.

One thing to address is the back elbow. For years, people have debated whether the back elbow should be up or down.

In reality, the key to the back elbow is not whether it is too high or not. The key is the wrist being bent and angled in a position of strength. This serves your swing in many different ways. First, it allows you to work straight back when you separate. It also keeps you from taking your hands too far back. When the angle of wrist is strong, it also produces a more direct move to the ball when you take a swing. Make sure the back elbow stays in line with the shoulders and not higher. If the wrist is angled properly, then the elbow will maintain a better angle. The tendency many players have when the back elbow starts down or angled is that when they separate, the elbow will move up and then it becomes detached from the body and causes a slam down into the ribs. The other thing that happens when the elbow is down is that you tend to lose the strong wrist angle and your swing doesn't come out as clean.

This is a great topic to study with MLB hitters. Watch games and video, studying their grips and wrists, as well as the back elbows. Most—if not all of the great hitters—hit with their back elbows up and even with their shoulders. Keep an eye on their wrist angles and see the similarities. The back elbows do come down to the sides, but the key is that the elbows do not initiate the swing. They work in unison with the sequence of the swing.

There are tendencies for younger hitters who have not gained total strength to want to stay inside the pitch so much that the back elbow will lead the swing almost in front of the knob of the bat. The top hand grip with proper wrist angle will help in this case.

Footwork

Footwork is the stepping stone to the swing, going a long way toward determining how consistent your swing is and can be.

Balance comes from the way your feet are aligned and where your weight distribution is in your feet. We have talked about where your weight should be in relation to the balls of your feet to help be in an athletic position. Now, as you set up in your stance, remember that if your feet are pointed straight ahead or inward that your weight will be more in the balls of your feet. If your feet are pointed outward, your weight will be more in your heels. It is much easier to maintain balance when your weight is in the balls of your feet, which allows for a better chance of producing a good swing.

The same thing applies when separating into your hitting position. When taking your stride through your separation, make sure the inside part of your front toe or instep lands on the ground first. Land with your foot fairly square and parallel to the front of the plate. Sometimes the front foot will be at a bit of a 45-degree angle depending on the flexibility you have in your front hip. When you land on the instep, it will keep your front knee pointing toward the plate and keep your front hip pointing toward the pitcher, which allows you to stay square or closed long enough to let the pitch get to the hitting area. This helps you be more direct to the ball with your swing. Some hitters think they need to open their hips to get their hands and bat head to the hitting area. The problem arises when they land too open with the front foot, then the front knee will point toward fair territory and will cause the front hip to open too early. This causes the swing to start out toward the plate and makes a hitter work around the ball, resulting in a longer swing.

Some issues that impact the front foot and how it lands are being late in your timing and getting your foot down when the ball is already in the hitting area. Another problem is created when you overload the back leg, which results in either rushing forward and landing open or getting stuck on the back leg. Still another issue is created when we are anxious or panic and we get tense and open up with our front side. Lastly, when we get overly concerned with pitches on the outside part of the plate or inside part of the plate, we try to cover those areas by stepping in that direction. Work to keep your front foot flat and planted as you swing. This will affect your balance and allow the back leg to work freely.

When taking your stride, be aware of the direction in which you are moving. Work to stay in the line with the pitcher as much as possible. If you are stepping in toward the plate or crossing over, check the following things that may be happening:

- Are you taking your hands behind your body when you separate?
- Are you overloading your back leg and then straightening it out, which makes your front hip turn in?
- Are you standing too far from the plate?
- Are you striding too far?
- Are you late with your timing?
- Are you standing too close to the plate?

Remember that your back foot will be a part of the start of your swing. Work your foot, knee and back hip together into the hitting area. As you start your swing your back foot should rotate on the ball of your foot and make a rotational move to allow the back heel to point up into the sky. Another way to think about it is to stretch the arch of the back foot as you turn into the ball. Apply what works for you and discard what doesn't.

Drills for success

All drills are designed to help individual hitters improve the mechanics of the swing. The absolute key with each drill is to use it with purpose. Drills are not busy work. As you develop your swing more in depth, you will gain a better understanding of where you are solid and where you need to improve. Every drill should be approached with one specific area to work on in mind. It is true that you can work on different phases of the swing through one drill, but the goal is to narrow it down to one part and put your whole thought process into it—one day at a time, one thought at a time and one aspect of the swing at a time.

Work drills for mechanics, but take it a step further and realize you are working on your mental approach, as well. Be present, be in the moment and realize that you are matching the feel of your swing with a thought. It is also good to work drills in sets. Start out working one swing at a time to be able to repeat. Then go to three swings. Remember the goal is to be present. Then go to five swings. As you work through drills, you will have good swings, as well as not so good swings. No matter the case, regroup and commit to what you are working to achieve.

No-stride swings: Understand that the swing works from the ground up. It's like building a house and starting with the foundation. A solid foundation will allow for better control of the bat path and swing direction. When you work no-stride swings, make sure to keep your weight even and solid. As you start the process, take your hands back and keep your weight at an even 50-50 proportion on each leg. When engaging your swing, work your hands and your pivot, backside in sync with your hands. This can be done off the tee, front side flips or in regular batting practice. Remember the main point is to keep your weight in the middle and not sway back. Keep your front foot firmly planted with your front heel stable and firm. Make sure that you create a solid

"L" with the back leg and hold the finish. Basically what you are doing is working backward so you can feel your finish and then work in the direction of your stride and separation.

Bottom hand/top hand drills: One-handed drills are a great way to understand how the actual swing works because it allows you to break the swing into two parts. Understand how the front half of the swing works and then understand how the back half of the swing works. Start with the bottom hand and make sure your grip is correct. Hold a bat that is not too heavy and can be controlled. A small bat would be great, but a normal bat will work as long as you choke up and make it feel lighter. Make sure your wrist is vertical and keep it in an angled position. As you work this drill, it's probably easier to start out with a no-stride approach to minimize the amount of body parts that are moving. Keep your hand close to your head in the stance position to control how far the hand separates back and maintain an angled grip. As you swing, make sure that the hand is working toward the ball, moving the front shoulder out as you hand works to ball. Keeping the front shoulder in will shorten the path to ball. You can refer to this hand move as "unfolding your arm." Then add your pivot as you move hand to ball.

Hip drill: This drill is a version of the bottom hand where you are working on hitting balls on the inner half. Starting in a normal stance, turn toward the second baseman if you are right-handed or toward the shortstop if you are left-handed. The main purpose of the drill is to work to separate straight and work to stay square. When you separate off the arm of the flip, land athletic and work to drive the knob down past your hip and hit down through the ball. This helps shorten your path and makes you more compact. As the ball comes off the bat, work to generate backspin and aim at the back net. When you complete your swing, you want to be able to hold your balance with a high finish. If you are falling back away from the hitting area then you are working uphill or are working around the ball. As you feel like you are repeating your swing, then begin to turn more to being square and repeat the same swing.

Angle flips. The main focus is staying square and working the bat path short and down through the ball. If you are working flips from straight on, move the person flipping toward the shortstop side about ten feet. A good alignment is even with where the shortstop is positioned on defense. For a right-handed hitter, the flip will be coming from behind. As you hit, make sure the front side stays in line with the pitcher's mound and then work to stay close to your body with the swing. Make sure you are working down through the ball, which will make you shorter and quicker. You want to work directly through the middle of the field and maintain your balance. For left-handers, the angle will be from the open side coming from the shortstop. Make sure to stay square to the pitcher's mound with your stride and front shoulder. Work the bat path inside and down through the ball, turning your pivot in sync. The direction is middle of the field and through the shortstop area.

Net drill: Set a tee against the side of the net about six to eight inches away. Measure yourself against the net about a bat's length. Work your swing close to your body, work short and stay inside the ball. Try to hit the ball parallel with the net toward the back end. If you work around the ball, you will tend to hit the net and not have a direct path toward the ball. The drill also helps you to keep your front side square, and your balance will be dictated by the proper bat path. For right-handed hitters, station a left-handed flipper close to the net on the left side. Vice versa for a left-handed hitter, as a right-handed flipper should be against the net on the right side.

PART 3

"Motivation is what gets you started. Habit is what keeps you going.

– Jim Ryan

"Watch your thoughts; they become words. Watch your words; they become actions. Watch your actions; they become habits. Watch your habits; they become character. Watch your character; it becomes your destiny."

– Frank Outlaw

"Don't stop when you're tired. Stop when you're done."
– Author unknown

Chapter 9

The Discipline of Motivation

The crowded, aging and foul-smelling bus pulled into the equally tattered and malodorous motel parking lot at about 4 a.m., screeching to a purposely-abrupt halt that awakened the handful of players who had somehow managed to ignore the stench of body odor and gas fumes to fall asleep during the drive. It had been a long game the previous night, followed by a long drive from one obscure map dot in the Midwest League to another ambiguous city.

Travel in the Major Leagues is magical, complete with first-class flight accommodations and four- and five-star hotels. Travel in the Minor Leagues—particularly in the lower levels like the Single-A Midwest League—is a completely different story. From the Beloit Snappers to the Burlington Bees, and from the Lake County Captains to the Lansing Lugnuts, travel in the Midwest League—or practically any other league at the lowest levels—typically involves long, laborious and late-night bus rides across multiple states throughout the Midwest.

On this particular trip, the players stumbled off the bus, and were given their room assignments and something to eat from a vending machine. Coaches instructed all of the players to go to bed quickly because the wake-up calls for the afternoon game later that day would come quickly.

Two American young men grabbed a key card, entered a room and promptly staggered into bed, neither one of them bothering to brush their teeth or change out of their shorts and T-shirts. Roughly 30 minutes later, a rhythmic, muffled pounding on the wall from next door awakened them. The Americans quickly concluded their teammates from the Dominican Republic were partying next door . The American young men were livid by being awakened at 5 a.m. They bounced out of bed and banged on the next door, imagining the scene behind the door and preparing for a confrontation.

When the door opened, however, the two Americans were stunned to see what was actually causing the sound. The two Dominican natives had taken one of the mattresses off the bed, propped it against the wall and were hitting soft-toss baseballs into the mattress. That, my friends, is the definition of hunger and the epitome of motivation! That's what it takes to be the best of the best.

So, what is it that gets you out of bed in the morning or keeps you out of bed until the wee hours? Why do you do what you do on an everyday basis? What is your goal for today, this week, this year, in 10 years? How do we see yourself in the future? We are getting deep and to the heart now. All of these questions are important to ask yourself in order to understand your life and what makes you happy. Whether your motivation is money, fame, love, companionship, sense of worth or sense of belonging, you must understand why you do what you do. The stronger your motivation, the better chance you have to succeed.

In baseball, motivation is probably the one thing that drives every player in their career. From a young Latin player wanting to make it to the Major League in order to make enough money to provide for his family to a player from

The Discipline of Motivation

Southern California wanting to become the greatest hitter who ever lived, motivation is the cog in the wheel. It is the oil to the motor, the water to the trees, the driving force to push you to work tirelessly and to endure any pain necessary in order to achieve your dream.

Often in baseball or any other sport, motivation is derived from the sheer desire to win or the longing to be better than another player. Other times motivation even comes in the form of jealousy, anger and resentment. Whatever the motivation may be, it can serve as the driving force to lead you to the action. Motivation will make a player work extra hours or take extra swings, watch more video, perform more reps in the weight room or invest more time on the mental side and how to control the little voice in your head. Some of the powerful effects of motivation are refusing to quit, refusing to give in, becoming more resilient or just exhibiting a "never-say-die" attitude.

Another type of motivation that players live by is enjoyment of the routine. We all live by some sort of routine as we go about our daily lives, and in baseball, it is one of the most important things you can do. Too many times players make their routines menial and mindless by simply going through the motions without giving their preparation routines any significant thought. A challenge for you is to work to be aware of every detail of your routine to make it more beneficial, but also to enhance your ability to stay in the moment and sharpen your focus. If your routine is to hit soft toss every day, are you willing to do it at 5 a.m. in a hotel room? And are you detailed enough to focus on every pitch in a ballgame, not just the overall results?

Your routine becomes your habit and then your habit becomes your way of life. Or to put it even more succinctly, you first make your habits; then your habits make you. Many successful players have a mindset routine that allows them to prepare successfully on a daily basis. When you are mindful of how your routine affects you positively or negatively, you can and should be able to adjust it as you see fit. Another challenge is this: If it's not broken, don't fix it.

An example of a good, solid routine is that of Texas Rangers outfielder Shin Soo Choo. He has a routine that he follows on a daily basis, regardless of whether it is a home game or away. For an evening game, he arrives at the ballpark around 12:30 in the afternoon and makes it a point to say hello to every person he encounters. He enters the locker room, changes clothes, answers texts or emails and goes to the training room to take care of any physical issues he may have for taping or stretching. By 1:30 p.m., he is in the batting cage starting his hitting routine. He will start off the tee, getting loose and then he moves the tee from the middle of the plate to the inside part of the plate and then to the outside part of plate. Throughout his tee work, he is mindful of the feeling of his swing and is open to talk about how he feels and his commitment to repeating his swing. On every swing, he is working to hit a line drive into the back part of the net.

After his hitting routine, Choo will grab a bite to eat and then go to the video room to watch that night's opposing starting pitcher, as well as relievers he might face. More importantly, he is watching the types of pitches he is likely to see, as well as identifying velocity. This is where he formulates his mental game plan for the evening. This takes about 45 minutes to an hour, as he may write notes as a subtle reminder. After the video session, he returns to his locker and prepares for batting practice, chatting with teammates about various things. Batting practice is about his timing and the direction he is working to hit balls, as well as his throwing program for arm care and his outfield play. He follows the same type of routine on road games, as well.

Obviously, when he has days where he doesn't feel as good with his swing, he spends more time in cage, as well as in the video room working to address specific issues. Overall, his routine is quite similar on a daily basis and serves to prepare him to be his very best every game he plays.

If you want to be a professional, prepare like one. Be aware of your routine and enjoy it. The purpose of the routine is to place yourself in a good, solid state of mind that helps you be successful. But be aware that a routine can be altered or adjusted by unexpected events. Don't be a slave to it. Remember that a routine does not define you or your performance. It only serves to help prepare your state of mind.

An area you want to be careful with is when your motivation becomes fear, anxiety or tension. These are emotions that can sometimes make you run away from challenges and negatively impact your performance. The fear of failure is probably the biggest problem that a hitter must face. It leads to so many negative thoughts and feelings, which limit the joy and fun of playing this great game. The reality of baseball is that failure will happen much more often than success. Failure can sabotage and cause doubts within every hitter. The important thing to remember is to accept failure for what it is, deal with it and move forward. Utilize a short-term memory approach. You don't have to like failure, but you do have to accept it and learn from it.

Remember this tidbit in troubling times: "The definition of insanity is doing the same thing over and over and expecting different results." Learn to make mental adjustments. Self-assess and ask yourself what you were attempting to do in your at-bat and what made you have a good at-bat or a weak one. Did your ego kick in and were you trying to do too much? Were you just trying to make contact? Were you intimidated by the opposing pitcher? Were you feeling like you had no confidence and had no chance? Were you trying not to strike out?

When you realize your state of mind and how it led to success or failure, then you can work to maintain or adjust it for the next at-bat. Sometimes it can be a mechanical issue you felt that led to success or a mechanical flaw that led to a weak a- bat. A strong suggestion when dealing with mechanics during a game is to make sure you know your swing well enough to be able to commit to that tweak. Otherwise, rely on your game plan or approach to make the adjustment. Your state of mind is the only thing that you have 100 percent control of 100 percent of the time. Sometimes adjusting mechanics in a game could lead to over thinking or "paralysis by analysis."

Above all, believe in yourself. Your value is the product of your thoughts...on the baseball diamond and in practically any other endeavor in life. In the mathematical equation of baseball and life, you need to remember this formula: Add to your self-worth and maximize your results by multiplying the positive affirmations you tell yourself. Conversely, you will subtract from your potential and minimize your results by multiplying your insecurities. And ALWAYS remember this: The little voice inside your head will go further toward determining your success or failure as a hitter than any coach, any drill or any routine ever could.

CPSIA information can be obtained
at www.ICGtesting.com
Printed in the USA
FFHW010919301018
49155496-53368FF